Broken Pieces
Created My Purpose

Broken Pieces
Created My Purpose

Earica Alexander Cole

Eara's Girls Media Group, LLC
PO Box 2488
Valrico, FL 33595
bookearicacole@gmail.com
www.earicacole.com

Library of Congress Cataloging – In Publication Data is available upon request.

Printed in the United States of America

Design Cover by Nailah Narcisso-Jones
Text Design by Earica A. Cole
Cover Photograph by Jaleesa Collins

ISBN: 979-8-218-12715-2

First Edition

"Great things come from work and perseverance. No excuses."

Kobe Bryant

DEDICATION

This book is dedicated to my beloved uncle, Apostle Joseph Lee Brown, who played such a vital role in my life. He died on November 20, 2022, but in so many ways he will always be with us. He was a great man of God, a father, a grandfather, a brother, and an uncle. Thank you, Uncle Joseph, for the prayers, teachings, love, and guidance you provided to me for the last 45 years. We miss you! We will always miss you! I love you!

CONTENTS

INTRODUCTION

Wow…what a journey! Sharing so many intimate details of my life throughout this book was scary. I was so nervous when I first started this process, but that feeling is long gone and I now feel FREE! Free to tell my story to the world.

For the last few years, I have been struggling with if I should even write this book. I knew it would mention a lot of pain that I had buried deep inside, a long time ago. I also didn't want to give people the opportunity to criticize my life experiences based on a book even if it is my truth. After a lot of prayer and talking with my family, I decided to tell my story. I decide to lose any care for judgmental people and focus on all the women and men this book might help.

I wanted to focus on the people who needed healing because that is what I had to do. I had to heal from so much! There have been so many broken relationships, broken promises, and fragmented dreams in my life that I barely knew where to start with my story. Once I started writing, I realized that in each situation, I had learned something. Instead of giving up, I healed, and I soared. I am better because of each of those situations, and I was inspired to do more along the way. While writing my memoir, I also realized that I was rescued when I didn't even realize I needed to be. My purpose was defined.

Because I now understand that purpose, I could not wait another moment to tell you my story.

I also wanted to share the power of love with you. Not just to be loved but to love others in return. I am so thankful and blessed that God gave me two wonderful parents, Jerome, and Eara. The love and values they instilled in me as a child, shaped the person I have become today. As a child they ensured me that I was not only loved but also protected.

I did not always understand why my parents were so strict when I was growing up, but I understand now. It was their way of protecting me. Today as a wife, mother, and business professional, it all makes sense. My heart is filled with gratitude to both of them and everything they taught me. Although my father is no longer physically with me, his teachings and encouragement are often loudly ringing in my ears. My mother is getting a front row seat to see how I pass and fail some of life's test. She always encourages me to do what's right, which doesn't always align with what I want to do. She is still mothering me and teaching me how to be the best version of myself in every situation.

My parents knew that my life would be filled with triumphs, failures, celebrations, heartaches, love, and pain. They also knew what I know now! I am certain that with God in my life, all things are possible. He is the light in our darkest hours. If we trust him and lean into his understanding rather than our own, we will always know that even things that happen that we perceived as "bad" will work out for our own good.

Come with me as I take you through my journey that I once thought was bad. Yes, it was hard sometimes but it was worth it. It was the key to unlock my door to happiness. Let my experiences be a lesson of love for your beautiful purpose in life. You too are worth it.

Broken Pieces

Created My Purpose

CHAPTER 1

SUGAR FOOT

I am grateful for the love and life God has blessed me with. As I am writing these words, I feel so much gratitude. I am grateful for everything good and everything bad that has happened in my life. I look at the bad experiences as lessons now. Those experiences taught me to never make the same mistakes. The good experiences are reminders that I am loved and that my village is strong.

Since, I was a little girl; people have told me that I am spoiled. This is possible, but what I really know for sure is that my God blessed me with two wonderful parents. If they spoiled me, it was out of love and wanting the best for me. My daddy, Jerome Alexander, passed away in 2005, but I still feel his presence. I feel his love every day. I am blessed to still have my momma, Eara Alexander Simpson, to love and be loved by her. It is the love of my momma and daddy that has sustained me over the years. It is my prayer, that I have brought them the same joy that they poured into my heart and soul.

They were both previously married and had children with their first spouses, so I am my momma and daddy's second daughter. My sister Kathy and I have the same mother. She was thirteen when I was born, and she also "spoiled me."

Kathy was so excited about having a little sister, but she was worried. We laugh about it now, but she was not excited about bringing me home. The problem was …I was born with eleven toes. Yes, I've always been an over achiever! Kathy wanted them to remove that extra toe before I left the hospital. The doctor tied some type of string around the toe, and it fell off over time. Of course, we still laugh about that too, but Kathy was a really worried little thirteen-year-old. She went to Momma's hospital bed and said, "Momma, what do you think about that baby with all of those toes?" Momma hadn't seen me yet because she was asleep when they delivered me. She panicked and asked to see her baby. Lesson learned! Never let your thirteen-year-old daughter see your baby before you do.

Momma said I was not home long before my eleventh toe fell off, but she knew that something else was wrong. I cried a lot, although I was not wet or hungry. By the time I was a toddler, those tears turned into screams. Screams of pain. They knew it was not a mental health issue or learning disability because I was talking like a five-year-old. I was also learning to read and write at an early age. I was not behaving badly, and I was doing well in every area of my development until the pain started.

Momma and Daddy also noticed that I had a great memory. It was almost photogenic. They would read picture books to me, and I would remember every word from each page based on the pictures. I would sit in a chair and repeat the entire book as I turned the pages. That was on my good days -- the days when I was not in pain. On a difficult day, I screamed and cried.

My parents–took me to several doctors in Jacksonville, but nothing seemed to help. The doctors didn't know what was wrong with me, and they misdiagnosed me numerous times. Momma would tell the doctors about the pain in my arm. At some point, one had the bright idea to put an arm in a cast. The cast was placed on my arm when I was around five, but that too was painful. They said it was "growing pains."

Neither the cast nor any medication helped me. Because my parents did not know what was happening to me, Momma was never too far away. During that time, she worked for a bank as a customer service officer. She would take off as needed, until one day they told her she couldn't have the day off. My dad said, "quit!" Daddy was an executive at Southern Bell, and that meant he worked long hours and made good money. His salary allowed Momma to come home to be with her baby at all times, I really needed her.

When Daddy came home from the office, he filled my face with kisses and told me everything would be okay! He called me his "sugar foot." That was his name just for me until the day he died. He kept a close eye on his "sugar foot." They all watched over me and cared for me, including Kathy.

During doctor visits and wearing the cast, my Aunt Cynthia, one of Momma's sisters, came to visit. After seeing me in so much pain she told Momma to take me to another doctor. Aunt Cynthia thought she knew what my condition was because she had seen this behavior of screaming in pain before. Her son, Rico, had sickle cell anemia. She insisted that Momma have me tested right away. Finally, a doctor gave my parents the proper diagnosis. I too, had sickle cell anemia. I was only around 5 years old when they received the news. I did not know what sickle cell anemia meant. Momma and Daddy were both tested, and they had the trait. I was diagnosed with hemoglobin SS. My parents were crushed. It's an inherited disease that clogs blood vessels and cause severe pain. It can also cause organ and tissue damage.

This is also when all the rules and restrictions started. All the things I was told I could not do came home with us and stayed the rest of my life. Even as a child, I refused to listen to those rules. I wanted to be a normal kid. I couldn't play sports, but they allowed me to become a cheerleader and do other activities like ballet, gymnastics, tap and clogging. Yes, I was a clogger. Momma and Daddy wanted me to be happy, but I know now that they were terrified. When a parent hears the words "sickle cell anemia" or "incurable disease," it must be hard. During that time, many statistics showed that the life span of people with sickle cell anemia is around 40 years.

I remember my cousin Rico coming over to talk to me about both of us having sickle cell. He was my favorite male cousin, and he was more like a big brother, so I believed him when he told me we would be okay. He said we had a superpower. Because he was so cool, I believed that too. I wish what he told me had been true for both of us, but he passed away in 2011, at age 40, from sickle cell anemia complications. I remember our final conversation in his hospital room. He told me that I had great work ahead of me and that God would use me to change the world. He was passing the mantle of strength to me.

Rico's death broke my heart. I felt like I lost a piece of me. My big brother and one of my biggest supporters, was gone. In addition to my grief, I was scared. I was afraid that I would die young too. Would I live past forty? Rico was right, and the statistics are wrong in some cases because I am still here to tell my story. God has a plan for me, and I am grateful for every day on this earth. Because my cousin is gone and I am still here, I know exactly how blessed I am. I do not take that for granted. I live and love with everything inside of me.

Many years before Rico passed, my parents knew that I wanted to live my life to the fullest. They knew I didn't want to live every day as a patient. I just wanted to live. Momma and Daddy wanted me to be happy. Although I wasn't allowed to play sports, I continued to thrive and experience many diverse activities. I am grateful that they exposed me to different extracurricular activities so that I would feel like a normal child. Even though I loved to dance, I never mastered clogging, ballet, tap or gymnastics. Because I loved music, Momma would buy albums for me, and I remember dancing around the house like it was my personal stage. I also had a passion for singing, so Momma decided to put me in voice lessons. I was in the chorus in elementary and junior high school. I was also in the church choir throughout school. I loved to perform, and my parents learned early on that I was not shy! If there was a talent show or pageant, I was always ready to participate.

In the seventh grade, I decided to run for Miss Eugene J. Butler. This was a contest at the seventh-grade center, I attended. That is when I learned about competition, and how friendships may change amid competition. I learned life lessons that I apply even today. I also learned if you want something, you better work your hardest to get it.

I worked hard to win that night. When I was announced as the winner, my family went wild in the audience. Daddy was crying because he was so proud of me. Kathy was in the back helping me change for all the segments. I was too young to understand what she was going through that night. Earlier that day; she buried her dad. She left his funeral and came home to be with me. I can't even imagine burying one parent and attending to the needs of someone else hours later. But that's who my big sister is to me. Thirty plus years later, she would do the same thing all over again. She has always put my needs before her own. Now that she is getting older, I don't allow her to do that as much, because it is my turn to take care of my big sister.

That night and so many fond memories from my childhood still make me smile. I also had experiences that were hurtful and stayed with me over the years. When you are a child, it takes you a minute to realize that the outside world is different from your home life. Unfortunately, when I was young, I learned what racism looked like before I turned ten years old. I was an innocent little girl, who believed that all my friends in the neighborhood were the same, but I couldn't have been more wrong.

My father's salary in corporate America meant we could afford to live an upper middle-class lifestyle. That lifestyle meant a nice home. Our dream home was not in a neighborhood with a lot of people who looked like me. I attended a private elementary school, Trinity Christian Academy, from pre-school through to the first grade. I was always the only black child in my class, and I would ask my parents why. I can't recall the answers that were given to me, but I understand now because my niece is living the exact same experience. They wanted me to have the best education, and also to be able to compete on all levels. What my parents didn't realize until I explained was that I was not welcome. They would often paddle me, and my parents initially were okay with their disciplinary structure, but it seemed to become obsessive.

I remember on several occasions, kids asking me why my hair was "poofy," or why I didn't wash my hair more often. Although it may have been curiosity, it made me uncomfortable. They made me feel that there was something wrong with being black. Like I was strange. Momma and Daddy finally realized that me attending Trinity was harming my self-esteem, and they decided to transfer me to another school with a little more diversity. In the second grade, I attended Jax Heights Elementary. Although the demographics there was still predominately white, there were minorities who were being bused from the other side of town. Sure, I was getting a good education at Trinity, but I was missing learning about African American culture. Did my parents make the best decision? I'm not sure. Maybe I missed a more competitive learning advantage, but I know that being around more people of color made me feel safe as the beautiful little girl I was.

No matter what was happening at school or on the playground, when I entered the doors and safety of our home, everything was normal again. I can say today that there is nothing normal about being the only person of color in your class and feeling completely isolated. There is nothing normal about being on the playground with children who do not want to play with you because of the color of your skin. There was nothing normal about little white girls wanting to know why you had so many ponytails and they have one.

Even some of my teachers treated me differently. There was an unfortunate situation during my second-grade year. I scored the highest amongst all the second graders at my new school. But my teacher, made a lot of fanfare about the second runner up, which was a white student. When I went home and told my parents, Momma decided to have a meeting with her immediately. I sat in the car with one of my friends while Momma was talking with my teacher. I remember watching Momma walk quickly out of the school doors and the teacher running behind Momma in panic and waving her hands. I later learned what she said to my mom, "Do you think I treat Earica differently because I think she's a nigger?" Yes! She uttered the word before she knew it. God protected my teacher that day! He protected her from Momma and protected Momma from going to jail. Momma and dad never reported her, and I never asked them why until writing this book. My momma said, the teacher was running behind her and begging her not to tell. She was so sorry, and she said she would lose her job. I can tell you that after that day, she was the nicest person in the world to me. She was the first person to ever refer to me as a nigger, but sadly she would not be the last.

Like many people of color, I experienced racism at school as well as on the playground. I will never forget my neighbor, a little white girl, who we will call Little Miss Katie. Little Miss Katie's parents had a pool in their backyard for her and her friends. Well, I was her friend too as long as I didn't try to get into her pool. Black children were not allowed! We all played hide and seek together and rode bikes, but when it was time to swim, I was told to go home. I am not referring to a year during segregation; this happened in 1984! We could talk outside her home, but I could not go in her home nor stick my black feet in her pool. I didn't even know how to spell the word racism, but I was devastated the first time she invited her white friends over to swim but did not invite me. I told my parents that Little Miss Katie said I could not swim in her pool. I do not remember what Daddy or Momma said. I do remember the look on Daddy's face. He did not rush over and curse her parents out or make a big deal out of the situation in front of me. They comforted me with hugs and love. Now, you've got to understand who my dad was as a person. My daddy was a hell-raiser if you rubbed him the wrong way. He didn't care about a person's status or location; if you messed with his family, there would be trouble. Within a couple of weeks, the next noise I heard was construction workers in our backyard. They were putting in a swimming pool just for me! For me and all the kids to enjoy whenever we wanted to. Well, except for Little Miss Katie.

All my parents ever wanted, was for their girls to feel loved and protected. They wanted all children to feel equal. My parents did not purchase the pool to be boastful. Their actions were saying, "I will protect you and give you and your friends a safe place to have fun. Your skin color doesn't define your abilities or your character. Whatever you want in life, go for it. Don't allow anyone to treat you different." The other lesson I learned from them doing something so special, was to work hard so that you don't have to settle. I am so grateful for every kiss, every hug and of course, my pool. I am grateful that they taught me to not want a seat at the table but to own the table instead.

My father wanted to go above and beyond for us because he was raised in extreme poverty. My dad was one of nine children and was raised by a single mother. I was told that my granddad shot a white man trying to protect himself. In those days, men of color were sent away by train to other parts of the country for their own protection. My granddad was sent to California from Bartow, Florida when my dad was young. My dad hadn't seen his father in over 30 years until we traveled as a family to California when I was around twelve. I'll never forget my granddad crying uncontrollably while meeting all of us and seeing my dad. That was the only time I ever spent with him. A couple of years later, he passed away. I didn't attend his funeral, but my father went to say goodbye one last time.

Long before his father died, my dad watched his mother struggle, so he wanted to provide a better life for his family. He would tell us there were somedays he went to bed without eating. He was a football star in high school and decided to go to college. He then enlisted in the navy and later graduated from Florida State University with a master's degree. He was big on education and felt that with a good education, you could make your own trail regardless of your race. He had suffered so much pain in his life that he didn't even want to discipline us unless it was about our school lessons. He let Momma handle things when I got out of hand.

Momma lived quite a different life from my father as a child. My dad was always teasing Momma, saying that they were rich. My grandfather, Zed, was a pioneer in the Church of God in Christ. He founded the church in Midway, Florida and traveled throughout Florida teaching and preaching. He was also a sharecropper and sold a variety of fruits and vegetables. There are so many stories of how he made money as an entrepreneur to provide for his wife and eighteen children. You read it right, eighteen children! My grandfather was married to his first wife and had nine children. During childbirth, his wife passed away and he married my grandmother and had nine more children. Momma was number twelve in line.

Both of my parents' families are extremely close. Their closeness taught me to love and cherish my sisters and their children. Every month I'm at a baby shower, wedding, birthday, or family celebration. Education is also important to

Momma's family. There are several doctors, lawyers, entrepreneurs, and educators throughout, so there aren't many conversations about are you going to college. Typically, it's what college are you going to? Although Momma never finished college, she has owned numerous businesses. She taught me hard work and not sleeping on your potential. I know she regrets not finishing college, and that is why she pushed her children so hard. It is my hope that there is someone in your life to push you too. Most of all, my hope is that there is someone that will love you as much as my parents have loved me. I hope this chapter and the following chapters will show you shining examples of what simply loving a child can do to give them a good foundation. We all deserve that! We can all love and be loved, even if we were denied that as a child. It is my belief that if given the proper tools, we can heal from so many things. Oftentimes, we just need to believe in ourselves and have someone else believe in us. My parents believed in me. I believe in you!

CHAPTER 2

HOT GRITS

I was a daddy's girl, but my relationship with Momma will always be unshakeable. In addition to an unbreakable relationship with Momma, I am also grateful to be a wife, stepmother, sister, and friend to people who love me as much as I love them. All those relationships are so important to me, but in this chapter, I would like to speak to you about sisterhood.

I make it clear that I have six sisters, but I only have two biological sisters. As I explained in chapter one, Kathy and I have the same mother. My other biological sister, Terri, also known as Shay, passed away in March of 2020. Shay was five when I was born. Momma also had a son, Lopez, with her first husband. Lopez died from meningitis at age two, and Kathy was only five at the time. Momma rarely mentions Lopez, but I know it is still painful for her. My other sisters, Trinnett, Trina, Delores, and April, are my god-sisters. "God" is the perfect name to put in front of sisters much like the women in my life. Only God could have created and protected the bond that we have. It is a blessing and honor to do this thing called life with them by my side. We are all so different yet still so similar because our common goal and intentions for each other are the same. Our goal is to always put God first. After that, we strive to love and support each other.

The oldest of our sisterly tribe is my sister, Kathy. I promise you that Kathy thinks she is my mother too. The story about Kathy not wanting to bring me home until I got rid of the extra toe is so funny because 45 years later, she is still concerned about my well-being. Our age difference automatically made Kathy the commander in chief and that is just the way I like it! I am so grateful that God blessed my life and my company, so that I could hire Kathy as the Chief Operating Officer for my businesses. She takes her position very seriously, but she takes our sisterhood to heart! We talk and text all day, every day! Even if she were not my COO, we would still talk daily, that's just the kind of bond we have. That is just the way it has always been. That is the way it will always be. There are times I'm more comfortable talking with Kathy than Momma or anyone else in my family. Momma shares information with her sisters that she would never tell me, so I realize it's just a part of our strong sisterhood.

So many things have happened to Kathy that would have broken most people. I watched my big sister experience trauma when I was young. Not just once but several times. Her first husband stood over her and discharged his gun twice. The shells were found at the crime scene but not the bullets. We were horrified when we found out what had happened to her. A few months later, she was working at GMAC when a mass murderer came onsite and killed everyone in her department. The only reason she was not murdered is because Kathy was relieving the receptionist at the time, so she wasn't at her desk. Let me change that sentence. The only reason my sister is alive today is because God moved her from danger. She is a walking testimony! I often tell her she needs to write a book, because she has so much to share that would help people. Through all of it, she has been such an honorable and courageous woman. Her resilience is unmatched.

I wish my relationship with Shay had been the same as my sisterhood with Kathy. Sadly, our relationship was the complete opposite. From what family members have told me, our relationship was strained from the day I was born. Even at five Shay wasn't happy that her daddy was having another baby with his new wife. I do not blame my sister for what she was feeling at five years old. There were adults (meaning my dad, Momma, and her mother), who set the tone for our relationship. As much as I love my dad, I have to say he set it all wrong. He loved Shay so much that he would do anything to make her happy. Early on, when she came to visit, he let her do whatever she wanted to do because he was always trying to make up for lost time. Being a holiday and summer parent was difficult. He wanted to make sure she knew how much he loved her. He never told her no, and she would kick and scream to get his attention. In the end, it did all of us more harm than good.

I did not know my relationship with Shay was strained until I was around 7 years old, and she was twelve. I just knew she argued with my dad a lot. I did not dare talk back to my Daddy or Momma, but Shay was just the opposite. She said whatever she wanted to say and expressed her anger every time she came to visit. I was too young to understand all her anger, until it was thrown at me. I mean literally thrown at me.

Shay came to visit us often, and I looked forward to seeing my big sister. She was so funny, and we would make up rap songs together. She told me she was a famous rapper and I believed her. She also had a beautiful voice. I was happy to see her after Kathy went off to Bethune-Cookman College because I felt lonely without my other oldest sister.

One summer, when Shay came to visit, she was put in charge of the house and me while my dad was at the office, and I am sure Momma was at the church. The house rule was no company when Momma and Daddy were away. The minute they walked out of the door, Shay broke the rules and had boys and girls in the house, partying and having a good time. She did not fix breakfast, so I was hungry, and I called Daddy and asked if I could make myself some cereal. He asked why I did not eat breakfast. I told him I did not eat breakfast because Shay had company and she did not cook. He asked to speak with Shay while I rushed to the kitchen to make cereal with his permission. Shay was so mad after she talked to Daddy. She told her friends to leave, and she went in the kitchen to start making my breakfast. She saw me sitting at the countertop eating cereal, but she didn't say anything to me. I ate quietly because I knew she was mad. After I finished my cereal, I got up to put my bowl in the sink and softly asked Shay if she was mad at me. That was a mistake! Before I knew it, she threw hot grits at me and missed. Not warm grits! Hot grits! I ducked, so the pot and the grits hit the kitchen wall as I ran to my parent's room and locked the door. I was crying and terrified as I rushed back to the phone to call my dad again.

Momma and daddy came home immediately and found me hiding in their room. Yes, I was hiding from Shay. Momma loved Shay, but on that day, she was furious and wanted her gone. Momma insisted that my dad pack her things and take her back to her mother. I watched in horror as Daddy packed her clothes and led her to the car. I've got to be honest; I was wondering why Momma didn't just spank her like she would have spanked me or Kathy. My dad wasn't a spanker, but Momma didn't play! That was the day; I started to understand being a biological parent vs. a stepparent in some households. I'm not sure if my dad or Shay's mother ever told Momma she couldn't spank their daughter or if she just assumed she couldn't. At some point, Momma got the message to keep her hands off Shay.

Shay left that day and our lives as a family were never the same. I was blessed that the grits missed me, and I was not physically burned, but her relationship with everyone in that house went up in flames. The trust was gone, and I do not think we ever got it back. My parents never trusted her to be alone with me again. There were no physical scars, but I was permanently scarred mentally from that moment. We were all scarred. We were broken and my sisterhood was hurt forever. Shay was scarred more than anyone. I believe she felt like my dad chose me and Momma over her and she never got over it. Just imagine being twelve and knowing one mistake caused people in your family to not trust you ever again. She must have been so hurt and felt so alone. For the first time, Shay was forced to leave her dad's new home. They had every reason not to trust her but that still hurt my sister. I am hurt just thinking about it while I write this sentence. Before that incident, I was a little sister waiting for my big sister to visit us again.

I do not remember how long Shay stayed away after she threw the pot of grits at me. I just remember how different it was when she came back. She would always pinch me if I did anything she didn't like. After the pinch she would remind me that I talked too much. My eyes would water but I never cried. I now realize that Shay felt like I took her daddy from her. He was her world, and she was daddy's little girl for five years and just like that.... he was gone. Not only was he physically gone, but he also had a new family and a new little girl. In her five-year-old innocent little eyes, I was the enemy.

Kathy never saw those moments because she was away at college when Shay visited, but like my parents, she never trusted Shay to be alone with me. Shay wanted to be a sister to us, but she didn't know how to. She struggled every visit. She was a trapped little girl trying to fit in. What she didn't realize is she did not even have to try because we already loved her. I admired how smart she was and how she knew she could be whatever she wanted when she put her mind to it. I admired her natural beauty. She had pretty hair, long nails, and a model figure. I wanted to look like her.

After the situation with the grits, every visit, Shay verbally and physically fought with our Daddy, and that terrified us. She would try to hit him and even bite him, and he would have to cross her arms and hold her until she calmed down. Shay had no respect for him or Momma as the adults in the house. She would go home and do the same with her mother, so they would bounce her back and forth throughout her teenage years.

The craziest part of all is that her visits and her behavior became a part of the norm for us. As far as Momma was concerned, Shay could visit, but, unfortunately, we all knew how the visit would end. No matter how hard my parents tried, Shay rejected what they offered her. Momma would make hair appointments for us both, but Shay always refused to go.

The bottom line was my sister felt rejected because of the situation with the grits so she rejected us. Now I realize she was always acting out of anger that should have been dealt with through counseling. I knew that things were not okay between any of us again, but she was still my sister. She will always be my sister. Momma would often just tell us to pray for Shay. She prayed for Shay and was concerned about what kind of life she would have. Every time my Daddy had to take her home, he would be visibly heartbroken. He wanted to spend more time with her, but it never worked out.

Now that I am an adult and a stepmother, I know that the grits incident was the moment when the adults should have gotten her help. Instead, the blame game started and lasted almost 40 years when really, we should have all been in counseling. Shay died feeling like an outsider and she was not! She was our sister! My father's oldest beloved daughter.

In between Shay's visits, God sent me four additional sisters to love. Kathy was still in college, so my parents needed a babysitter. Sadly, Shay was out of the question even if she was in town. Eventually my parents asked one of our church members if her twin daughters, Trinnett and Trina, could become my babysitters. Their mother said, "yes." She was such a sweet lady and took absolutely no nonsense. The twin's mother and my parents had a great relationship. She and my Daddy could argue or debate about the bible for hours and then laugh and high five each other. She wanted her girls to make some extra money that summer for school clothes and whatever else they needed. It was a perfect situation for all of us.

My parents often attended late night dinners and other events related to Dad's job, or church. The twins would spend the night in Kathy's room and take care of me. Do not ask me why, but for some reason, I thought I was in charge of my new babysitters. I was thrilled because I thought I had not one but two people to boss around. This is how one of my first encounters with Trinnett went as she was getting juice from the refrigerator.

Me: "You are not supposed to get anything from the refrigerator without asking me."

Trinnett: "Little girl, go sit down."

Ha! That was the end of that! It was also the beginning of almost 40 years of sisterhood and friendship with the twins. Number one, Trinnett put my little smart mouth in check. Number two; it was Trinnett who taught me that I had to respect not just my parents, teachers, and adults at church but also my friends, she taught me so much.

I do not know if Trina said anything that night as I marched out of the kitchen with my mouth closed. Trina was, and will always be, a quiet fighter. Trina taught me how to physically fight. We would wrestle like boys and had so much fun. Even when we were having fun, Trina would play to win. When we had pillow fights, she would help me gang up on Trinnett until she was in tears. Trina was my bestie in my head. We just got along so well.

After Trinnett set the tone for what our relationship would be, we really fell in love with each other. I had the kind of relationship with the twins that I had with Kathy, and the relationship, I always wanted with Shay.

In less than a year of coming into our lives, I realized the twins were more than my babysitters. We were a family and that is the how we treated each other. We would often sit around and sing gospel songs until the middle of the night. At every birthday party and slumber party I had, one or both were there. Soon, the twins started staying with us more. They would let me tag along for every school event when they were in junior high, and high school.

Momma and daddy asked the twins' parents if they could be their godparents. It was a big help to them, and it gave Momma a sense of peace about who was watching me. My parents fell in love with both and loved how they loved me as a little sister. Trinnett and Trina not only became Momma's daughters and my sisters, but they also became Kathy's sisters too. She developed a strong bond with the twins. A bond that they still have today. Soon, we no longer said God-sister, we just said sister.

I give them so much credit for being the best sisters they could be to Shay, but it was not easy. They had grown close in junior high school, but when trouble arose between Shay and my dad, she would be angry with all of us when she left, and we didn't hear from her until she came to visit again. The thing was, they had the option of not having a relationship with Shay once we were adults. I did not have that option, nor did I want it. She was my biological sister, and we were connected for life by blood and love even if it was partially strained. So, Kathy and my god-sisters had the option to walk away from Shay, but do you know what? They never did. They prayed for my sister and remained patient with her even when she was mad about the smallest things.

The strange thing about my relationship with Shay was, she never let anyone take me through the hell she would give me. I will never forget going to a high school game with Shay in her hometown at Bartow High. Momma and Daddy were both hesitant about letting me attend, but I begged them because I had never gone to a high school football game. Plus, when Shay was good, she was so much fun! We were at the game when this girl that didn't like Shay, bumped into me. Shay told her to apologize, and she said harshly, "no." Before she could say anything else, I saw Shay beat that girl like she had stolen her prize possession. The police officers literally had to pull

Shay off her. I was screaming and crying, and the police officers called Momma and Daddy to come to the school to pick us up. My daddy was so mad, but honestly, it was the moment I realized that Shay and I may not have the best relationship, but she wasn't going to allow anyone else to bother me. I know it sounds crazy, but I felt safe with her again. I felt like she really did want to be my protector.

No matter how much I wanted them to be with me, I was once again getting ready to lose not one but two sisters. When the twins graduated from high school, they were off to Florida A&M University (FAMU). Shay also attended Florida State University, which was my father's alma mater. Once again, I was the only child at home, but I was older now, so I wasn't lonely.

In true fashion, Kathy's bedroom did not stay empty for long. The next sister God sent into my life is my little sister, April. Her beautiful mother was a single parent, and we all went to church together. My dad and momma allowed me to start inviting April over to spend the night when her momma had to work late or attend events at our church. Just like Trinnett and Trina had been my babysitters, I now had the role of big sister, and I loved it. This was new to me, and it gave me a new sense of responsibility. Having a little sister gave me a sense of wanting to protect her. As the years passed, I realized April needed me as much as I needed Kathy, Trinnett, and Trina when I was her age. They had been there for me, and now God positioned me to do the same with April. I must remind myself today, that she's grown with two adult daughters because I'm still very protective of her.

April and I would go everywhere together. Football games, skating, teen clubs, and even movies. She was always down for whatever. We were together so much that people often thought we were biological sisters, and we didn't bother to correct them. April stayed over so much, that my senior year in high school, which was her freshmen year; she and I decided that she would move in with us so that we could attend school together. Our parents agreed. Honestly, my parents liked the fact that I was never alone with the twins gone, and her mother felt the same. April's father was such a fun-loving man, but he struggled with addictions. He loved April and called her "sweety bum." But sometimes, she would go months without hearing from him or seeing him. She grew to love my dad as a father figure, and called him "Papa J." My dad often reminded her that her father loved her, and that addiction is a sickness. When April's dad passed away in 1997, her family and mine felt that I would be the best person to tell her. That was hard, but, someway, God gave me the words and allowed me to be the emotional support she needed during that time.

The final sister to join our clan was Delores. I had already left home when Delores came to live with my parents. She also attended our church, and she was not living in the best environment. The first lady of the church asked Momma to help her. Momma's definition of helping a child, or young lady in need, is to move them in with us, feed them, clothe them and most of all… love them. So that is what Momma did. Delores was and she is still quiet and loving. I did not get to spend as much time in the beginning with her as I did our other sisters, but we are sisters, nonetheless. I was grateful that my parents helped her and grateful that she was with Momma while my daddy was sick and after he died.

Momma and dad were thankful that the twins were both in Tallahassee to "watch me" during my freshmen year of college. Trina was married with a baby, but Trinnett was single and living with her roommate. They both allowed me to come and go as often as I wanted when I needed space from my roommate. I often thought I was being slick when I needed to use one of their cars. Little did I know, they both knew exactly what I was up to! I always had to end up back at one of their apartments within a reasonable time. Letting me borrow their car was just their way of keeping up with me.

So, that is how our small family of five became a family of nine. This is how our sister circle grew from three to seven. I have learned so much from all these women. They taught me how to love and respect everyone. When you do not respect the people in your life, major damage is done. Trinnett simply asked for respect, and her actions created a lifetime of love. Trina protected me early on, and throughout the years I felt the need to protect her as well. Everyone knows the roles we are expected to play in each other's lives. Sure, we have disagreements from time to time, but we never stay angry with each other, not for that long anyway.

In addition to respecting your family and friends, you must value what they bring into your life. All my sisters are so different. We bring so many different things to each other that are valuable. I am easily the bossy sister, well, me and Trina. But I am only allowed to be bossy with respect. My sister Trinnett is prissy and the one who thinks she can cook better than the rest of us. My sister Kathy is our counsel in chief. We cannot argue long without Kathy stepping in to make us straighten out whatever we think the problem is. Shay was the outgoing sister. If you needed a laugh or a good time, she was the sister you would go to. There was never a dull moment with Shay. Now Trina is the sister who goes out of her way to give Momma the most attention. She checks in constantly and likes "her time" with Momma alone. There is no money in the bank to replace time. We all appreciate her for that. We call her the spoiled one. She is the compassionate sister. Delores is the quietest of all of us. But she is ready to jump in and help whenever needed. April is the life of the party, the comedian. She's stubborn, funny, and emotional all wrapped up in one big gift.

As the years passed, the respect and the value we shared turned into automatic loyalty to each other, as both sisters and family. The love Momma gave the twins, April and Delores created a mother-daughter bond. My father loved them just as much, but the mother-daughter bond was extra special. If something happened to Kathy and me, Momma would still have four daughters because they are loyal to the end of time. What I love about my mother's relationship with them is she never tried to replace their mothers. She loves and respects them for sharing their daughters with her. Because I was able to watch how my mother loved children who were not biologically hers, it helped cultivate my relationship with my bonus son, Bricen. Regardless of the bloodline, when you love a child with your whole heart, biology doesn't matter.

Our love and loyalty show up in everything we do. There is no... "I will see you all in a few years" when we are making plans. We show up for each other physically and emotionally daily. If one sister is happy, we all are happy, and we show up to celebrate. If there is pain, we show up for the pain. We have been there for each other during sickness, broken relationships, divorce, birth, and deaths.

Let me add that there were times when we were not showing up for each other. Most of the time, it was because one of us would be in a relationship that was given a higher priority, and that is fine. What is not fine is letting that relationship take you away from your family. If you are in a relationship with a person who cares about you, they will care about your family. Maturity taught us that, and we made a pact that we would never again stay away from each other because of a relationship, and that includes our spouses. When that agreement appears broken, we just must talk about it and get back on track. Communication is so important. You cannot hold the respect, value, and loyalty together very long without good communication.

What Shay and I did not become was good communicators with each other. We failed each other in that department. The feelings and anger she had towards my father were not our feelings and anger. We should have talked when we got older. We should have told each other how we felt and expressed our pain. Instead, that pain stayed with us and inside of us for over 40 years. As children, we would go weeks without talking. Those weeks turned into months as teens and years as adults. Just before she died, we had a major fall out, and we stopped talking. I saw her at an event in January 2020. The devil was telling me not to speak to my big sister. Oh, how I wanted to listen to the devil, but God pushed me across that floor into her arms. She was sitting with her daughter and a few friends when I spotted her. I went to her table and said, "Hey Shay! I just wanted to come over and say I love you." She looked up at me and smiled. "Hey Earica, I love you too." We hugged and I kissed her on the cheek. I also kissed and hugged my niece, who was sitting beside her. We hadn't spoken in two months.

I did not force the conversation because I thought those words were the beginning of our healing. Unbeknownst to the both of us, she only had weeks left on this earth. The words, "I love you" were not the beginning! Those three words were our final goodbye. Just imagine how I would have felt if she had left this world without God giving me those three words. God granted me that peace!

I want you to learn from my broken relationship with Shay. When things are wrong, do not be concerned about who was wrong or right. Walk across the floor and whisper, "I love you."

"Sisters make the best friends in the world." Marilyn Monroe

CHAPTER 3

THE NORTHSIDE

No matter how good or bad your family situation might be, you eventually must go out on your own. You must find your own place in the world. Along the way, I hope you meet good people and people you can call your friends. I also hope you find a perfect partner. Someone to love and someone to love you. I had to kiss a few frogs along the way, but God did send me my soulmate.

When I look back, I realize that my parents chose wisely regarding their friends and who they associated with. Church was a big part of all our lives, not just on Sundays but all the time. Because my parents played such an active role in church, of course we did too. I started making friends at church at an early age. Some of my "church friends" are still my friends, and as I told you earlier, some became as close as my family.

Of course, as I got older, I started making friends at school. The kids in neighborhood and school did not always give me the love I received at church and home. No, they did not all look like me, and yes, we had diverse cultural backgrounds. I was bused to school in the 6th and 7th grade to what was known as the black side of town, the northside. I loved it! I loved the culture, the music, and of course the boys. It was then that I was introduced to rap music. I loved JJ Fad – Supersonic and Salt N Pepper. It was there that I truly found myself. I was a young black girl, becoming a black woman. Although my best friend was white, I was meeting new friends that looked like me. I was learning my culture and enjoying. I was learning new things and dances that I hadn't seen before. It was there that I met one of my dearest friends, Keyona. She was from New Orleans and had a deep accent. Her father was in the military, and she had lived in various places. She was so smart and loved African American Studies. We just clicked! Keyona's family members treated me like I was a part of their family, and their house was one of the only places I was allowed to spend the night.

When I reached high school, I told my parents that I did not want to go to my neighborhood school that Kathy attended. I had done my research and the neighborhood school, Nathan B. Forrest High School, was named after a prominent Confederate Army general during the American Civil War and the first Grand Wizard of the Ku Klux Klan from 1867 to 1869. Momma and Daddy listened to me, and I went to Edward H. White High school where I was happy. Keyona attended Edward H. White too and we became even closer. I joined so many organizations, and I really felt a part of not only the school, but the culture outside of my home.

My sisters, Trinnett and Trina had attended Edward H. White, so I knew a lot about the school. They came from a large family and many of their relatives attended school with me, so I immediately had "cousins" that knew me and accepted me.

As much as I loved school, I learned some hard lessons. My entire life, I had been so loved, protected, and adored by my dad, so it was new to me to be around boys that didn't like me or respect me. I went through a stage in life where I wasn't confident in my appearance. You know that adolescent stage where everything on you looks awkward and weird? I'd been swimming almost every day during the summer, so my complexion was three shades darker. I sucked my thumb until I was thirteen and had to get braces because of an overbite. Plus, I was born with the Jerome and Eara forehead! Ha! So, I didn't feel like the princess Momma and Daddy told me I was. I didn't feel like that girl they had always treated like a princess. No matter what, I refused to let the boys or girls define me. There were girls who only associated with the girls in their clique. There were boys who only liked the lighted skinned girls with long hair. Let's face it, there are cliques in schools between boys and girls. Heck, there are cliques even when you are adults!

45

In the ninth grade, I joined an organization for girls called The Society Club. In tenth grade, I became the vice-president and by 11th grade, I was the president. Even though I was president, I really was not happy with the group. There were almost one hundred girls in the group, and we really were not doing much community service. I got tired of debating with the other girls about things we should be doing to better ourselves and others, so I started a smaller group my senior year called The Limited 20. It was in high school where I realized that I didn't need a large circle of friends. I just needed a few loyal friends who wanted to challenge each other and make a difference. Twenty-seven years later, I am still friends with some of the ladies who were in those groups. We have been together through high school, college, marriages, divorces; you name it, all because we were in a small group together as teenagers.

I share the story about starting my own group with you because I want you to know how important it was for me to create my own path. It is important for you to create and cut your path when a door closes on you. I was at the school where I belonged, and I was not going to leave or feel left out because of one small group of people. If I had let them bother me or hurt me, I would have spent a lifetime letting people tell me I did not belong.

My Daddy had already shown me, not told me, what to do when Little Miss Katie wouldn't let me swim in the pool, so that is what I was doing when I started my own group. I was too young to realize it at the time, but I was doing exactly what Daddy did. I was in high school trying to build a pool for all the girls who wanted to swim with me. Forming my own group laid the foundation for me as a leader and so many others. The Limited 20 made me not care so much about trivial things. It made me love myself more and allowed me to be around people who wanted to be around me.

After starting the group, I started to feel more comfortable about myself being a young black woman. Colorism is real but I was not going to fall into that trap. I was now in love with my brown skin. My self-confidence was beginning to mean something to me, and I learned that from my friend, Keyona. She was always so sure of herself, and I admired that about her. I still admire her; she remains true to herself and who she is.

As I started to try dating, I carried that self-confidence with me. There were guys who did like me and a few I had a crush on, but my daddy was not allowing me to date seriously anyway, so problem solved. To really put a fork in my dating life, Daddy showed up at school! Yep…he didn't just stop by to visit, he had recently retired early and decided to substitute teach at my high school! That was the worst! He let everyone know he was my Daddy. The boys thought he was a cool teacher, but Jerome Alexander put the fear of God in those boys. They would not even look at me. I was so mad!

Before Daddy arrived on the scene and before attending Edward H. White, I met a guy who we will refer to as Joe. He lived in Detroit but was visiting his family in Jacksonville that summer when we met. He ended up moving to Jacksonville to finish his high school years but attended another school. He was two years older than I was, so I was in the 10th grade when he graduated and went to the army. Do not forget Joe's name because we will come back to him later in this book. I did not seriously date Joe, but I did meet a guy my senior year, who we will call Travis, whom I was head over heels for. Travis was handsome, great dresser, and treated me nicely, but his dream was to be a rapper. When we met my senior year in high school, he was a freshman at Bethune Cookman College. My dad liked Travis, but he was not happy with his plans for the future and honestly neither was I. All I saw were the videos and rap magazines that just made them appear only about money, drugs, and disrespecting women. I didn't know any rappers, so the media gave me a bad perception although I loved the music. But my dad was thinking about stability and safety. He was always thinking ahead for himself and his family.

After graduation, I was extremely focused on getting ready to leave for college at FAMU. Travis was focused on studio time and performing at nightclubs. That was his dream, and I was trying to support him, but it did not work for me, so we broke up in the middle of my sophomore year in college. We just wanted different things out of life, and I realized I couldn't force him into what I wanted, and he needed to pursue his passion.

I loved FAMU, and there is nothing like going to a historically black college or university. The campus was filled with black professors and students, and don't even mention the band, sororities, and fraternities. My parents were happy with my decision to attend that university, so they were a little disappointed when I decided to come home to attend cosmetology school after my freshmen year. My roommate situation didn't go well, and I knew that my dad's health was declining. He had been diagnosed with chronic obstructive pulmonary disease, or COPD and Momma didn't seem herself as she tried to take care of Daddy. She was tired, so I needed to be there for them. I wanted to go home, and so I did.

My parents were not going to tell me I could not come back home. What Momma and Daddy were clear about was my education. They were not going to force me to stay at FAMU, but I still had to finish college somehow. That is when I announced that I wanted to attend cosmetology school. Well, that was fine too, but I still had to finish college, so I enrolled in Florida Community College at Jacksonville during the day and went to cosmetology school at night. In addition to attending school, I was doing hair for some of my friends at home and working for a tax collector. I wanted my own money and knew I had to work to get what I wanted. I felt like my parents' financial situation had changed. I didn't know what was really going on, but I would soon find out. All my life they drove Cadillacs and Lincoln Town cars. Now suddenly, they downgraded, and they were driving smaller, inexpensive cars. They were also cooking and selling dinners after church. So, I didn't want them to try and do anything extra for me. I later learned that my dad failed to pay taxes after early retirement, so it set them back once he had to start making payments.

In the midst of work, school and helping to care for Daddy, I met a guy who was wrong for me. I mean really wrong. He was not abusive, but he was too old for me. We were not living together, but he was at my apartment ninety percent of the time. My momma got sick. She was diagnosed with Hyperthyroidism. This was tough because I had never seen my mother ill. She was like superwoman to me. This was a time; I should have stayed focused on my parents not this random crush. I was going through my rebellion period and unfortunately, my priorities were misplaced.

At first, I saw it as love but quickly realized it was control. I begin feeling uncomfortable, so I started looking for another place to live. When the relationship went south, the person who really helped me end that relationship was Joe. Remember my friend from the summer before high school? Well, we stayed connected and wrote letters every few months while he was away in Germany. I could not tell my daddy how unhappy I was, so I told Joe. When I say rescued, I mean he sent me the money to help move me out of the situation and into my own apartment. Not only did Joe rescue me, but we also started dating. This is when I stop and tell you that most of the time, it is best not to start dating your friend! Before I knew it, I was in love with him. I will not say he didn't love me, but Joe was a cheater. I knew that because we had been friends for years, but I was that, "it will be different with me" girl. I had no idea that my relationship with Joe was worse than the relationship, I had just run away from. This new relationship was about to turn my life upside down.

It was hard for me to really pinpoint what was going on in the beginning, but I knew something was not right. I had never been around anyone with so many secrets. Secrets and lies. He wasn't shy, but some may say he was an introvert. He didn't let a lot of people into his life. But I learned it was because he was always hiding something. Correction! He was hiding everything! He was always on the phone when he thought I wasn't looking. He was always going in the bathroom with his phone. It was just one lie after another. I found myself living like a detective because I was trying to figure out what he was doing. I would always look at his phone to see who the last person he called. Just all kinds of foolishness. I was miserable!

In between what I thought were good times and misery with Joe, life stopped for me and my family. Daddy was diagnosed with chronic obstructive pulmonary disease, or COPD, in 1993, but by 1998 there were so many near death experiences. He had been a smoker since a teenager. In January 2000 he had an episode where he couldn't breathe, so we called rescue as we had done so many times before. But this time felt different when they picked him up. I had no idea that would be the last time my daddy would be home, but Momma knew. That was the beginning of a long hospital stay before his death. I remember Momma standing at the window singing an old hymn, "will the circle be unbroken." She felt he was not coming back to that house. Unfortunately, she was right.

My daddy had tricked me into moving back home a few months before. So, I moved out of the apartment, Joe had helped me find and went home again. I am so glad I did. It gave me more time with Daddy. He had told me if I moved home, he would stop smoking and get a lung transplant. The doctors told him if he stopped smoking for six months, he would be a candidate. Well of course he didn't stop, but I'm glad I was home to help Momma and Delores for those last few months. My dad had gotten me, and Shay hired with Bell South, which was formerly Southern Bell when he retired. I worked one exit from the hospital, so every day at lunch and when I got off, I'd stop by to see him. They had him in an induced coma for weeks. But I would still go there and just talk to him. We shared a love for football, so I would go on Sundays and watch the games in his room. He could not respond but he knew I was there and that's all that mattered.

A month after my dad was in the hospital, I was with Joe at a friend's house when I got a call from Kathy. She asked me to speak with Joe which wasn't unusual, but I could tell something wasn't right. She wanted him to get me to the hospital as soon as possible because Daddy was fading. I don't know why, but I insisted on driving. The controlling side of me took over. I grabbed the keys and jumped in the driver's seat. I got to the hospital and when I saw my dad, I realized he was alert. He looked at me and we cried like two babies.

Just a few days before, he had finally awakened from the coma and could speak a little. I hadn't heard his voice or seen his eyes in weeks! I laid on his chest and I remember him rubbing my head and telling me how much he loved me, and how proud of me he was. That was the day I grew up. I mean really grew up. I did not have Daddy anymore. I had to come of age! I was no longer "sugar foot." Even though I wasn't the eldest daughter, I felt like I had to take care of Momma. By now Kathy was not only married, but she also had children, but I was living home with mom. He shared some moments with me over the next few hours that I'll never forget. My daddy always said, "A man should never die alone," and he was not alone.

I didn't want to watch him take his final breaths, so I went in the waiting area with over twenty-five family members and friends and of course, Joe. Shay also had children and she was pulling herself together to get to Daddy from her home in Orlando. She made it just in time to say goodbye. After she left his room, she came in the waiting room to find me. We hugged and cried together. Our Daddy was gone.

CHAPTER 4

GIRL! DON'T DO IT!

After Daddy died, I was in a daze for a while. I missed my Daddy! I still miss him. The week before my dad died, Joe asked him for my hand in marriage while we were visiting him in the hospital. I did not know anything about this conversation until Momma told me after I was engaged to Joe. My dad was not the man he used to be physically or mentally at that point, but he refused to answer Joe. Momma said it was strange. He just stared off and ignored him. My daddy, superman, the one that raised me and could smell a rat ten miles away, would have sent Joe packing.

His funeral is still hazy to me. I do remember being angry. Angry that he left me. Angry that Daddy would not be there to walk me down the aisle. He wouldn't be there for my graduation or to see my children. I just wanted him back here with us. I know this sounds silly, but I was so mad at the repast when people were talking, laughing, and enjoying the food. It seemed so disrespectful that people were happy and taking pictures, and we had just buried Daddy. I was glad when it was over, and I did not have to talk to anyone outside of our immediate family. Even before the funeral I was upset about the process. Planning his funeral and worrying about what colors everyone would wear was absurd to me. I remember Kathy and Momma just telling me they would figure it all out. Shay went back to Orlando the day after dad died. She wanted to be with her kids and husband at the time.

That is what grief looked like for me. Boy did I grieve. I guess in some ways, I still grieve for him. To this day, I do not like repast services. I think it takes away from the family being able to grieve the loss of their loved one. It's more about making the guests comfortable. I also recognize that during grief, I prefer to be alone. I don't like a lot of interaction and people constantly asking me, "How are you doing?" I want to scream; HOW DO YOU THINK I'M DOING?

In some way, planning the wedding kept me from being totally depressed. No matter what I did, I still missed my daddy. I did not have his voice in my ear to help me make decisions anymore, but God showed me all the signs I needed to see to make a good decision and not marry Joe. Yet, I married him anyway. I can only say that if my Daddy were alive, he would have stopped my engagement to Joe. He was gone and not there to protect me. I needed his protection.

I think planning my wedding helped Momma with her grieving, but she also was about to be thrown into the madness of who Joe really was. In the midst of planning the wedding, less than seven weeks out, my godparents moved me and all my stuff to Arkansas were Joe lived. The next morning, I learned about a woman who he had been cheating on me with. She called while I was lying beside him. His awkward speech and pauses let me know it was another woman on the phone. Once I learned about the woman, I took a taxi to the airport to go back to my Momma in Jacksonville. This was before 9/11 so guests were able to meet people at their gates. When I arrived at the airport in Little Rock, Joe was at my gate. I told him not to come near me or I'd scream! Momma received a call from the mother of a girl Joe was fooling around with that same day. I was so heartbroken and just needed Momma to tell me everything would be okay. The woman beside me on the plane tried to console me as she saw me crying uncontrollably. Momma picked me up from the airport and broke more shocking news to me. She told me that the girl Joe was fooling around said she was pregnant. I was crushed!

This cannot be happening! I was planning to spend my life with this man! Momma was preparing one of the biggest events my family and friends had ever seen. We had spent tens of thousands of dollars and were expecting over five hundred guests. What will people think? What will people say? Joe kept calling Momma and I, but my phone was off. I asked Momma not to say anything to anyone and to allow me to figure it all out. I just crawled in her bed and did not want to move. After three days with Momma, Joe showed up to her house. He caught a plane to come and try and fix things. There was a silly part of me that thought I needed to know if he loved me. I was listening to my heart instead of my brain! Joe denied having an ongoing relationship with the girl and claimed he did not think she was pregnant. He told me he would deal with it, and I would never hear from the girl again. I took another week to decide whether to move forward with the wedding.

Well, I married Joe. It was one of the saddest days of my life. I was so emotional, and people thought I was just upset because my dad wasn't there. Truth is, I kept thinking, what the hell are you doing? I was in my dressing room with my friend, Keyona. She knew all the ins and outs of my relationship with Joe. She knew about the cheating and how I had doubts. Most of all, she knew me. Keyona knew that I loved Joe, and she knew I was in trouble.

"Earica, if you do not want to do this, don't. Do not marry him! Girl! Don't do it! I will pull my car up to the front door of this building and we will leave right now. To hell with these people!" That was my girl! She was all in and had my back in whatever my decision was. I did not tell my sisters because honestly, I knew they would no longer like Joe.

"I can't. Momma has spent so much money and time on this wedding. Over five hundred people are here. I cannot cancel now. It will be okay. He said it would never happen again."

I should have thrown that dress in the trash and ran off with Keyona like we were Thelma and Louise. But I stayed! The wedding was beautiful, and I made myself believe I was happy that day. In fact, I was so miserable. Joe was trying so hard to be super attentive. He had flowers waiting for me in the reception hall. He asked to speak with my mom, his mother, and his dad after the ceremony. It was the five of us in a room together. Joe cried and apologized to all of us for the hurt and disappointment he had caused. His parents were devastated because they were great people and were rooting for us. Momma adored him. He was always the perfect gentleman, and she felt he had just made a mistake. It was not a mistake. It was exactly who he was, and I knew it.

Joe's wedding gift to me was a honeymoon in Jamaica. I somehow managed to convince myself that I was happy there too, but I was not. Even on our honeymoon I was asking him about the other woman who said she was pregnant. Just imagine having that conversation on your honeymoon. He kept saying, let's move forward and stop looking back. He promised me he'd never hurt me again.

What have I done? What have I done? That is the question I kept playing over and over in my head and heart. Keyona's mother told us in high school; when a man shows you who he is, believe him! She was right!

We were not back home a week when the other woman resurfaced. I was on the college campus attending my new school as a senior when she made herself known. I walked back to my car from class where she had left a note. I was in Joe's jeep, yet she knew it was me and not him. She wanted to let me know that she was still seeing Joe. Her message was, "call me." I smiled while reading it because if she was watching me, I wanted her to see me unbothered. But in reality, I was furious! I went straight to his office, and once again he denied talking to her. He denied it, but I did not believe him! Not for one minute!

Oh my God! This was my new life! I had so much regret! I am telling you this story to tell you that this is not happiness. What I was experiencing is called settling, that's right. I was settling for a relationship with a man who I was in love with, but who was not in love with me. We were already friends, so maybe he did love me, but not as his wife. I am sure about that now. Maybe he was too young and not ready for marriage. The one thing my second marriage has taught me is when you love your spouse, you do not do things to cause them constant pain. Yes, you will make mistakes and have problems, but being married to Joe was different.

This is the crazy part... I got along very well with him. We both loved sports and having fun, he adored my family, and I loved his family very much. Imagine living your life with a person but never trusting them. We spent almost five years of having fun one day but fighting and arguing the next day. I caught him cheating so many times that I can't even count. I would yell and scream and ask him to leave. He left twice, and I left him once. But we always got back together. His family and my family were both trying to help us and keep us together, but it was useless. My life was a wreck! My heart was a wreck. In late 2004, that wrecking ball hit a steel wall and my life finished falling apart.

You see, I thought if Joe and I moved from Arkansas to Florida closer to family and he changed careers, he would stop cheating. Boy was I wrong. You can take a dog from a pound, but it's still a dog! It got worse! Every anniversary, I learned about a new affair. That was always the present! I kept asking myself why I did this to myself.

In 2004, I was planning to go out to dinner with some family and friends for a friend's birthday celebration. Joe announced he had to work late so he could not join us. There was nothing unusual about that because the one thing he never did was try to keep me from spending time with my family even if he could not make it. I was miserable, but I always found joy when I was with family.

What I thought was a night out on the town, turned out to be the beginning of the end for my marriage. While we were all standing around in the Cheesecake Factory waiting to be seated, guess who walked in? Joe! Not only did I see my husband, but he was not alone. There I was face to face with him and another woman. This time I was not alone! Thank God! Not only was he cheating again but he was humiliating me in front of my family and friends. Although some knew what we had been going through over the last few years, they were truly fighting for us. They wanted us to make it as a couple. Me telling them something was one thing. Now they witness it with their own eyes. He had taken cheating to a new level, or a new low, whatever you want to call it. Whatever it was, it broke me!

Joe was so busy cheating that he did not even ask me what restaurant I was going to with my family. He also did not care if he ran into my friends. Yep, so busy trying to get to that woman that he forgot about his wife being out and about. Just reckless.

My mind went blank, and my heart sank as I confronted him. I just lost it as my aunt pulled me away. Joe followed us outside and tried to explain. The woman ran away. She was clearly embarrassed. I'm not sure if she knew he was married or not. All I heard was him telling my aunt the woman was a friend and he needed to talk to me. It was like the scene in the *Sex in The City* movie when Big stood Carrie up at the altar. When he tried to talk to her, her friends grabbed her in her wedding dress, and they pulled her away.

I did not have any flowers to beat Joe over the head with, but I was capable of doing anything to him. My aunt stopped him in his tracks and told him I was going home with her, and I did. I have thought about that night one thousand times since 2004. I do not mean I thought about him. I think about how badly it could have ended for me. I thank God every day that I was with my family. I cannot imagine what would have happened if I had been alone and walked in the restaurant to find my husband with another woman. Forget them… I think about the rage that I would have been in and the damage I could have caused. That damage could have destroyed me, and they would have been my victims. Ladies, this is where you pause and read that last sentence again. Just think how terribly wrong things could have gone that night. God protected me from me! My God surrounded me with family, and my praying Aunt Vera, for a reason. My uncle and aunt being there made all the difference in my response. Initially, I was totally humiliated that so many were around. But now I know that's how it had to happen to protect me. They would not let me go crazy, no matter how much I wanted to.

The fact that my family members were there also, meant they had seen enough to help me move on, and that is what I did. I moved in with my aunt and uncle for a while. There was no way I was living with Joe ever again. Even Momma said to me and Joe that she was no longer telling me to stay and pray. She felt I had been through enough, and she did not want that pain for me that she had experienced with her ex-husband, Kathy's father.

After about a mouth, Joe realized I was not coming back, and he moved out and I went back home for a little while. It took me a long time to get over that hurt and shame, but my family knew, and they were holding me accountable for my next move. When you suffer in silence and tell people half of the story, they really cannot help you. Everything, and I mean *everything*, was out in the open now. There was no more lying about my marriage being okay! No more hiding that Joe was cheating! Crying myself to sleep at night was exposed, Thank God!

I had also told my sisters what happened, and I was relieved that my horrible marriage was out in the open. Now I had to decide what to do next, and I did not have to do it alone. My family was there for me. After a few months, I started thinking about leaving Tampa. I just needed a change.

A few months later, I broke the news to my family that I was taking a position in New Orleans as an Area Manager. For months, I had traveled back and forth doing the training for a merger. It helped me cope with the reality that my marriage was over and accept being "single again." This was a promotion that was right on time for me mentally and spiritually. I also needed the additional income if I was going to live the life; I had grown accustomed to living. Joe and I were not rich, but we were a hard-working young couple who were doing well for people our age.

Everyone was sad that I was leaving Florida, but they were happy I was getting a fresh start. For months, I continued traveled back and forth and stayed in a hotel. I would spend two weeks in New Orleans and two weeks at home. In December 2004, the company I was working for asked me to relocate to New Orleans permanently to run four branches from the merger. I accepted the position after a couple of months, but still traveled back and forth to Tampa until they found someone to replace me. Finally, I had had enough of living out of a suitcase. My long-term goal was to buy a house and move Momma in with me. Little did I know, she had plans of her own. Momma had reconnected with her high school sweetheart, Marvin. Lord, that is another story, but let's get back to me moving to New Orleans.

By February 2005, our divorce proceedings had started as I was preparing to move to New Orleans permanently. I did not want to talk to nor run into Joe. I needed a fresh start. He knew by me accepting this position I was really done. We did not argue and it went smoothly. I still loved my ex-husband, but I just did not want to suffer anymore. I moved on and carried that pain with me to New Orleans. Sometimes, you just must move on and carry the pain until it goes away. If you do the work on yourself, I promise it will go away.

In July 2005, my divorce was final - I was relieved. I went back home and packed up everything I owned and moved. I put most of my belongings in storage, and settled into my new apartment in Slidell, Louisiana which is only 20 minutes from New Orleans. I was still hurting, but it was good to be away from Joe. I really loved my new job, and for the first time since marrying Joe five years earlier; my life was calm again. Well, that is what I thought! I was so wrong! It was just the calm before the storm!

CHAPTER 5

THE BRIDGE THAT WAS BROKEN

I fell in love with New Orleans. I loved the city, the people and most of all the rich culture. Everything about New Orleans is beautiful even when it is one hundred degrees outside. The people who were born there loved the city more than I ever could as a new resident. It is one of those cities that most natives don't leave. Even if they go off to college, many return because it's that beautiful. Storms, threats of hurricanes and massive flooding has never scared or kept the natives away too long, but Hurricane Katrina changed everything. August 28, 2005 will stay with me and thousands of people in this country forever.

Like everyone in the country, I was watching the news on the August 26th and 27th. I was thinking that the storm looked bad, but I did not panic. As a member of management, I checked on my team at work, and everyone was okay. We closed the offices that Saturday to allow those who needed to evacuate to do so. It was a hard decision because, of course, people were trying to leave town, and they wanted cash. We just could not stay because we needed to do what was best for our staff. Most of the staff were New Orleans' natives, so hurricanes were nothing new to them. Being a Florida native, I had experienced my share of bad storms too, so I was not scared. I thought everything would be okay. Boy was I wrong. Everyone was wrong.

After my team assured me that they would be fine, I went out and purchased lots of snacks and started planning to binge-watch television for the next few days. I did not panic, but my Momma did. Let me tell you something about the term "mother knows best"! That is a fact! By the morning of the 27th, Momma was calling me every hour on the hour. She was watching the news and telling me she felt I should leave. She had sold her house two days before and was packed up to come move in with me. She stopped in Mobile, AL which was where her boyfriend, Marvin, lived. "This is bad," she kept saying. She told me my Uncle Joseph said, I needed to get out of there and she needed to come get me. Uncle Joseph was everyone's father in our family. He later called me and asked me to go where my mother and Marvin were. He said if the power went out, everyone will be worried if they could not reach me. When he speaks, you listen.

Later, that day, she called again and then she kept calling. Everyone was calling and telling me to get out of New Orleans.

Finally, Momma said, "If you don't get in your car and come here, I am coming to get you." She meant that.

I still felt I would be okay, but I did not want Momma to worry so I packed a weekend's worth of clothes, and I left New Orleans late that evening. I was convinced that I would be back in a few days. So that was it. I walked out that door believing I was coming back. Momma and Marvin met me at a hotel in Mobile, AL. Momma was so glad to see me. I could tell she was shaken, and the fear I heard in her voice went away. Shortly after checking in, the power went out in the hotel. I was so annoyed! my battery on my phone was low, and it was raining so bad that I couldn't get to my car to charge it. We had planned to get something to eat but decided to just go to sleep and wait for the storm to pass. By this time, all our phones were dead. We woke up and decided to drive farther east to Pensacola, FL to Momma's sister's house. It was so hot in the hotel and there was still no power. I wanted to drive west to go back home! She told me to get over it! I was not going home yet. When we got to a nearby gas station, we heard people talking about the devastation in New Orleans. We had no idea that New Orleans was under water. I was devastated thinking about all the people left behind. We found a nearby hotel and checked in. I quickly turned on the news, and I sat with Momma and Marvin as we watched in horror as all hell broke loose in New Orleans. It looked like the end of the world was unfolding on live television. When the levees broke and the water started to rise, I realized we were watching people drown. It was overwhelming as we watched the death toll rise with the water. My sadness turned to anger when I heard several news anchors referring to the victims of the hurricane as refugees. These were people of color who were also American. How did we suddenly become refugees?

I had no time to waste on anger. I just started praying that my friends and my staff were okay. It seemed like the storm would never end. No one's phones were working. I either got busy signals or filled voicemails. Several days passed before I found out that my some of my staff were okay. I didn't know if they were alive. It took over a week to hear from several of them.

When I think about it now, I am so grateful that we closed that bank and sent everyone home. I am grateful that Momma insisted I come to Mobile. I will never forget August 28, 2005, for as long as I live. I will never forget that almost two thousand people died, and most of them were people of color. How could this be happening in America? Would this have happened in Beverly Hills?

The next day, I called the Tampa Corporate office. All the executives had been waiting on my call. They wanted to make sure I was okay and wanted me to help them check on our employees in New Orleans. After a few days, I reported back to work via telephone and started to help any of the staff members that needed aid. On September 12th, I physically reported to the office in Tampa as a fill-in manager at one of the local branches. I continued to try to help my staff who were displaced. Many were in Houston and Mississippi. Our company provided financial assistance to help all of us relocate to hotels outside of New Orleans. That is when I learned how much the natives of New Orleans really loved that place. No one on our team had to stay in New Orleans, but some of the staff refused to leave.

I will always have respect for the company I was working for at that time. They took good care of us and helped us relocate. But honey, many stayed in New Orleans and wanted to rebuild. That organization did so much for the victims. I remember feeling so grateful for each leader. They taught me what servant leadership meant and looked like. I was new to management, so it was a defining and teachable moment in my career. By October, the company decided to relocate me to Ocala, Florida to run the three branches there. I was not happy about moving to Ocala, but New Orleans was no longer a viable option for me.

The second surprise I got that month was Momma married Marvin! Hold your seat because again, I will tell you that full story later in this book. For now, I will just say the newlyweds moved in with me. It was strange to have Momma and her new husband living with me. I only wanted my momma with my daddy but let me tell you something... MOMMA WAS HAPPY! So, there I was watching the newlyweds, and living in little Ocala with no love life. You cannot make this stuff up.

The truth is, Marvin, who died in 2016, was a good man. He was hurt about my current situation, and he wanted to help me rebuild my life after the hurricane and divorce. I didn't need money, I needed love and support and he helped Momma provide that for me.

In late October 2005, I decided it was time to go back to New Orleans to see if anything was left in my apartment and storage. No one could really confirm the status because the employees at the apartment complex and storage unit were displaced too. Momma, Marvin, and my godparents were not going to let me go alone. I had watched the whole city engulfed in water for over 60 days, and now it was time to face what I dreaded, but I had to see it for myself. I did not know what I would find at my apartment, but I was more concerned about my storage unit. My most precious belongings were there while I prepared a permanent home for myself. We stopped at the storage unit first because it was located off the highway two exits before the exit to my apartment.

There was nothing that could have prepared me for what I saw when we got closer to New Orleans. I was trying not to be upset about material things, but the human side of me was more powerful than the spiritual side when I saw my storage unit. I was crushed! Daddy was my first thought. All my pictures and everything he had given me over the years were gone. I did not cry! I sobbed! I had a trunk filled with precious memories. Momma and my godmother tried to comfort me, but there was nothing they could do. I did not care about my furniture. I cared about my memories with my Daddy. I wanted nothing else from that storage unit.

Momma and my godmother went through my belongings, and they saved what they could, but there was not much to save. The water had gone down, but the storage management had already warned me that my storage unit had sat under nine feet of water for weeks. Everything was covered in mildew and had a horrible smell.

After we left the storage unit, I tried to pull myself together for what we may find at my apartment. Even after watching the devastation on the news, you just feel different when you are one of the victims. That is what we were, victims! Not of a crime but of a storm! I was shocked to see a portion of my apartment complex ruined. The first-floor apartments had been totally under water and my neighbors who lived there lost everything. Each apartment was completely gutted out. It was awful to see all their belongings piled up on the street waiting to be thrown away, like they were nothing but discarded trash.

My apartment, on the other hand, was just the way I left it. We walked around in what felt like slow motion. The inspector had come in to access the damage and had thrown out all the food in the refrigerator for health reasons. Only the shoe boxes in the top of the closet were out of place. They had somehow fallen on the floor. We packed my things into the truck Marvin had rented and said goodbye to Slidell. We could not drive over to New Orleans to see the damage. The bridge was broken into multiple pieces. That bridge was really a symbol of what had happened there. Like that bridge, lives were broken. Some were broken into pieces that could never be put back together.

The rest of 2005 was filled watching my happily married mother and stepdad and a lot of television when I was not at work. I was not complaining because, after New Orleans, I was glad to be alive. Momma reminded me daily of how blessed I was. I had enough money, from my insurance and from my job, to start over, and I started thinking about my next move. What I did not have were my precious memories from my dad, and I had to try to move on without them. I started to think ahead as much as possible. I considered staying in Ocala, but I was so unhappy there.

I knew I was safe because I had God and Momma and Marvin for support. The thing I did not have was a social life, but that was about to change too. After the storm, family and friends contacted me to see if I was okay. One of those old friends was Travis, my high school boyfriend! Yes, the rapper! He did not make it as an artist, but he was doing well and living in Atlanta. Travis was a breath of fresh air for me during that time. We picked up right where we left off and started dated again. I could not say it was serious, but I felt alive again. I was happier. Our rekindled relationship did two things for me: It helped me forget about some of the trauma of Hurricane Katrina and I was not thinking about the pain Joe had caused me daily. We were getting along so great that I decided to move to Atlanta in May of 2006. Yes, I took an $8,000.00 pay cut and a demotion. I knew the position as Assistant Manager for a well-known Atlanta credit union, would leave room for me to grow, and I did. It was their largest branch and I felt I could deliver on bringing life back to the location.

Well, there was room to grow at work, but my love life with Travis went nowhere. His job transferred him to Ohio the same month I arrived in Atlanta. I am forever grateful to Travis for just being a good friend. A person I could truly trust, even if it were for a few months. When I think back to reconnecting with Travis, I realize that it was just God's way of bringing me to the place He wanted me to be. This was the place I would thrive professionally and personally. A place that would eventually change my life forever. Remember, some relationships are seasonal and not all of them are meant to be forever.

CHAPTER 6

I CHOSE ME

After Travis left Atlanta, I was wondering if I had made the right decision. I missed the fun we had together. I missed him and there seemed to be a void in my life. In an unhealthy way, I started to think about Joe again, but he was not a part of my daily thoughts anymore as time moved on. When I thought about him, I thought about how much time I had wasted on him. After he cheated the first time, I should not have wasted another day with him.

Have you ever thought about the amount of time you wasted in unhealthy relationships? Would you say you have wasted days, weeks, months, or years? Some people believe everything happens for a reason, and nothing that happens in your life is a waste of time. Many people believe that they learn something from every experience. I believe that both can be true in some situations, but my stronger conviction is… do not waste too much of your time on people or things that are not working for you. In the voice of writer, Demetria L. Lucas, "Don't Waste Your Pretty." Listen… she is right, and I learned that valuable lesson from firsthand experience. It is a lesson that took me five long years to learn; five years that I should have been doing something different with my personal life. The lessons I learned scared me for a very long time, and they are lessons I want other women to learn without taking five years to do so.

This book is neither gender nor age specific, but this chapter is for the young women, because we tend to stay in relationships when we know we should go. I am sharing this with you because some of your best years as a woman are during your twenties. Your twenties are your season of finding your womanhood. During this season you will most likely move into your first apartment or new home away from your parent(s) and their rules. Most of you will fill your days with the excitement of a new job, brunch with a friend, attending weddings and for some of you… giving birth. Yes… it is the time to party, take girl trips, and have great date nights. By your late twenties, life gets a little more serious; or at least it should. I am not saying throw away the fun, but I am saying do not waste your precious time, your beautiful body, your mind and your heart on things and people who are not serving you what you require the most.

It took me a minute to get that message, but for me it was crystal clear when I finally got it. I have already told you about my first and failed marriage. Now I want to elaborate on the moment I CHOSE ME! The moment I truly set myself free from Joe after dating, living apart, getting back together, and getting married, getting divorced and most of all… heartbreaks over and over again.

Now it is 2006 and here comes Joe. So, I'm getting settled in Atlanta, and out of the blue, he starts calling me again. Of course, he knew I had moved to Atlanta, and I'm sure he was made aware that Travis lived there at one point. It's funny how the "ex" always knows when you are seeing someone. But the crazy thing is, some of those old feelings came rushing back out of nowhere. He didn't beat around the bush. He simply asked if he could come to see my "new crib" and check up on me. My head was saying, "Girl, don't fall for it," but my heart was thinking – maybe Atlanta would be different. Really Earica? Do you really think Atlanta would be the best place to bring your lying, cheating ex-husband where there are seven women to one man? I responded, "yes, you can come." We started planning activities for the weekend including dinner that Friday night and going to Six Flags the next day. I did not invite him to spend the weekend at my place, but I did pack my overnight bag just assuming I would end up back at his hotel. Ladies, you know that bag I'm talking about!

We made plans to leave my car at his hotel and ride together. When I arrived at the hotel, there he was! He was standing in the lobby waiting for me! I got the same butterflies I used to get whenever I saw him. Or maybe it was a panic attack now that I think about it! If it was not a panic attack, it should have been one. I should have panicked and ran like my clothes were on fire the minute I saw him. But no, I didn't run. I got in the car and felt some more of whatever was floating around in my stomach. I remember what I was wearing and what we talked about as we drove to the restaurant. That was the beginning of our "let's get back together weekend." He was apologizing for not being there for me during Katrina and how hard it was for him knowing I was displaced.

Let me tell you how wrong I knew it was to be with him. I didn't tell anyone, including my sisters, that I made plans with Joe. I didn't tell Momma or my aunts. I did not tell anyone because I knew they would lose their mind after the hell I had been through. I just wanted to enjoy my weekend and think about the future! Deep down I knew I was being foolish. When we hide things like this, we already know what the end results will be. We just try to save face. I'm so thankful that social media wasn't a thing during this time. I could imagine my silly self-posting selfies for the world to see how ridiculous I was being. We see it every day, don't we? That friend or family member who has shared all the heartbreak they've experienced with a partner one week, and two weeks later she's posting how wonderful he is and how happy they are together. We can't wait to see what they post the next month. They call it manifestation. We call it insanity!

I made small talk with him as we ordered all types of appetizers. Looking across the table at him made me consider that, just maybe, we could try it again. He's always been charming. That only lasted for a few minutes. While we were talking about old times and what the future might look like for us, he received a text message. He glanced down at the cellphone and I glanced at him. He quickly told me that one of our mutual friends said, "hello" as he texted someone back. Let me tell you something…I knew he was lying! Lies! Lies and more lies! That text message to him felt like God texting me! It was that "get up and walk out" moment! It was that "don't be a fool your whole life" moment. I did not physically walk away at that moment, but my heart and head were running out the door, down the street and back to the safety of my home. It was nothing he said, or I said, but it was the way I felt. It was simply a text that snapped me back to reality. The old feeling of someone trying to kill me softly and emotionally. Kill who God made as a whole woman! I could not wait to get away from him!

I took a deep breath and pulled myself together as he continued replying to some chick as if it were someone who we both knew. As he finished lying to her, I stopped lying to myself. Everything that had ever happened between us in the past, flashed in front of me as he put his phone away. Every memory of times I lowered my standards and checked his phone when we were married came rushing back in my head, and most of all... back into my heart. The feelings I experienced when he would sneak into the bathroom to talk to someone, came back. I physically felt myself sinking to that small person again. I felt less than the world I had rebuilt with the help of God and my family. That woman who I smiled at every moment was just fading in front of me. Those memories and that horrible feeling of insecurity rushed inside of me and trapped me at that table. God no! I was not going to be trapped again. Because I didn't say anything, I do not think my ex even realized what was happening. We continued to talk and make plans, but my mind was a million miles away. I was physically having an out-of-body experience. My mind left the room, but my body was physically still at the table. I just kept listening, and every now and then, I would say something as he continued to talk. This time, he was not the one lying. This time, I was lying because I had no intentions of ever seeing him again. I was done!

Ladies, there is nothing like having a moment of clarity. A light bulb moment! A come-to-Jesus' moment. Whatever you want to call it, let me tell you how it happened for me and what it felt like. When you get there, you will know. I knew that now all I had to do was get out of that restaurant and away from Joe. I did not have the time or energy to debate or listen to him lie about the text message, so I did not even mention how I felt. I am not good at pretending, but that night I deserved at least two Oscars.

I just kept talking and walking to the car after he paid the check. I made small talk in the car. When we arrived at his hotel, I am sure he was shocked because I did not give him any indication that I wanted to go upstairs with him as we said good night. I had my pride and my overnight bag with me as I drove home in silence. I had my dignity in the front seat with me. I was so proud of myself, and I was not letting that go!

I did not get on the phone and call a girlfriend to tell her what happened. I did not even call one of my sisters like I would normally do. The very reason I did not tell them about my date is the reason I did not call them. They already knew who he was and calling them to confirm it again would not serve me or them. I just kept driving like I was escaping from someone, but no one was attacking me. I was just free, and I was driving back to my freedom.

When I got inside my house, I realized that I physically felt different. That old me had tried to return and I did not like it. I did not like her. I was not allowing her back! That Earica was gone! Without wasting another second of my life, I said what I had never been able to say to him. - "NO!"

When he called to see if I was home safely, I said, "thank you for a nice dinner. It was good to see you, but I do not want to do any of the activities we have planned for the weekend." The silence was our goodbye. He finally spoke and told me that he understood. It did not matter if he understood. I understood. I understood that my heart was not supposed to be broken all the time. I refused to go back to that feeling of not trusting the person I loved; the person who said they loved me. I was not going back to the pit in my stomach that made me cry at night. One text had snapped me out of five years of pain. One text! I wasn't mad. I wasn't disappointed. I was finally free!

That one night was just the beginning of knowing who I really am as a person, as a woman who loves herself. Earica Alexander was back and now had full control of her life. The next morning was the real test for me. In the past, I always struggled saying "no" to Joe or telling him it was over for the one hundredth time. That morning was different. I woke up truly knowing that I am supposed to honor myself and allow others to honor me. Saying "no" to my ex was not a split-second decision! It was what I meant! It was real. I had matured and come into my own.

I realized the difference between how I felt before and after he looked down at that text message. The voice of loving me said, "Earica, you are not here to be unhappy. You are not on God's earth to be insecure." Ladies, I do not know when your light bulb moment will happen for you. I do not know what it will look like, but I can tell you what it will feel like. You will feel free and happy! You will know what Dr. Lucas meant when she said that your pretty is important, so do not waste it.

Now here is the real beauty of what happened in that restaurant. I had to finally be released from that situation because God was preparing me for an unexpected transition. But sometimes, we miss what He has for us because we are holding on to the past. Even holding on to anger and not being able to forgive. I was no longer bitter about my divorce. I was finally done! I knew he was not the man for me.

I had no crystal ball to know that Brian was about to enter my life. Plus, I didn't care at that moment. At that moment, I didn't feel the urge to have a man, and I was not afraid to be alone. I was ready to love ME again. That release was beautiful, and it was intentional. I started dating me. Going to the movies and out to local sports bars, meeting new people. I was finally laughing and loving life again.

I didn't have a plan with another person. I just chose me! I want you to choose you. That is what I want for all young, beautiful women and men. That is what I want for the widow who is looking for a new mate or the newly divorced woman looking for love. I want you to love God and yourself so much, that nothing or no one will block you from real love and peace of mind. Choose You!

CHAPTER 7

LET'S DANCE

Can I ever love again? The answer to this question is YES! You can love again! You can be loved again. I was about to learn all about loving again.

I loved my new job in Atlanta, and I started to meet women my age with successful careers who became my good friends. Of course, when you live in Atlanta, friends and family are always visiting. I loved the night life when I was not hard at work and too tired to go out. One night, in late June of 2006, I was out, with my sister April and my cousin Tisa, at a popular nightclub. They both were in town to visit me, and we were planning to paint the town red. While entering the club, one guy just kept bumping into me. I was like, "Dude! What's the problem?" He grabbed me and said, "well since you want my attention, let's dance!" When we were not dancing, we were talking. That guy was Brian. He was the reason God brought me to Atlanta. I was dancing with my future husband and did not even know it! When you are in the club, you are not looking for your husband. At least I wasn't. After my first bad decision, I was feeling more like I better find my next husband at church. From the first night we met, Brian was focused on me. Everyone was just having fun and dancing with difference people, but not Brian. He was only dancing with me. We would talk a while and then dance. That went on all night, and we just connected in a nice way. He also shared with me that he had a son. I could tell immediately that his son was his everything. He pulled out pictures of him. We exchanged numbers, and that was the beginning of a beautiful friendship.

Brian was a breath of fresh air. We spent quality time with each other, and he made me laugh a lot. He too was recently divorced and transitioning to being a single father. I was loving my job, and things were really going well financially. I had used my insurance money, from the property damage during Katrina, to invest into a few rental properties. I could see the wheels turning in the right direction. Life was beginning to feel good again. Meeting Brian, not even a year after my divorce was final, was freedom. I knew that I wanted to one day be someone's wife again and to have a family, but I was taking my time this go around. I thought after my ex moved to Ohio; I would just enjoy the single life in Atlanta. But Brian and I had a different kind of relationship from what I had been dealing with while married to Joe.

It was that night in the restaurant with my ex-husband that cleared my path to happiness. That was God closing one door and opening the windows and doors in my house of happiness. I did not rush into my relationship with Brian. We were both newly divorced and were at the point of knowing that a rebound relationship would not work. We just wanted to have fun! No drama, and no forced commitments. I also realized that the reconnection with Travis was only the path to Atlanta, and that relationship was not going to work either. Joe and Travis were my past, and God wanted to show me He had something better in store for me. He had a mate waiting for me, and that man was Brian. We just took our time and enjoyed each other, but he was different. When I say different, I mean he courted me!

After many dates that led to a romantic relationship, I realized something so important in any relationship. I trusted Brian! When we were together, I was not in a bad mood the way I was with my ex. I was not worried about who he was with or what he was doing! How refreshing! When I was with Joe, I was always looking in his face to see if he was lying, looking at his phone to see who the last woman was to call him, checking emails to see who he was communicating with. Miserable is the word for it now that I reflect on him and our life together. When I looked in Brian's face, I saw a man who was glad to see me. He hated infidelity just as much as me. I recall wanting to see a movie where the storyline was about unfaithfulness.

He was clearly disgusted. Someone who understands the sanctity of a union, had finally walked into my life. Some of our initial conversations, once we decided to be exclusive, were if you ever feel I'm not enough, let me go. Don't cheat on me!

Brian was not perfect then or now, but he was perfect for me. When we met, he was an entrepreneur, owned his own home, and was about his business. He wanted to be married to someone he could trust because he was trustworthy. Please read that sentence again. I want you to read it again because when a man wants you, you will know. Not only will you know it, but you will also feel it. I didn't feel this prior to marrying my first husband. I knew exactly what I was getting. A cheater! There's that saying again, "when a man/woman shows you who they are, believe them."

You do not deserve to be in a relationship with someone you cannot even trust on your honeymoon. You do not deserve to be in a relationship with someone who makes you feel like you need to check his/her phone every time they step in the shower. I never want to live like that again, and I hope I will write enough in this book to break that cycle for you if you are living that way.

When I realized who God sent to me, I was all in. Brian was all in. In addition to falling in love with him, I fell in love with his son, Bricen. You could not love Brian and not love his son. That was a deal breaker for him, and I do not blame him. It was beautiful to be around a man who looked at his child the way my parents looked at and loved me. Their bond made me even more attracted to Brian. He was only two years old when we met. Not only did he have a great relationship with his son, but he also had primary custody of him, which I admired. Brian's mother also lived with him, and that was something else we had in common. No one loves their mother more than I do, so I was thinking, "he is a really good guy." There were challenges along the way, but I was not wrong. Brian is that guy I would want as a friend if he was not my husband.

For the first time in years, I was happy with my personal life. Brian and I met dancing, and to this day, we love to dance together. Work was going well, and the organization saw the highest growth between June and December of 2006 due to my branch. At that point, I was promoted to Staff Development Manager. Of course, that included a raise.

Not only were things going well at work, but I also started to buy houses in Atlanta to be used as rental properties. I look back at 2007 as a wonderful year for me professionally and financially. Like all things beautiful, you wake up and find bumps in the road to happiness. That is what happened with Brian and me. Thank God, we made it to the other side, but it was not easy because by 2008, the country was facing a recession. Now, I had tenants who could not pay their rent.

After 3 years of rebuilding, I was facing financial trouble, and I needed help. My investment properties were failing because my tenants were getting further and further behind on their rent. I will explain all of that to you in my chapter about finance, but right now I want to tell you Brian's response when he realized I was in trouble. First, I had so much pride that it took me months to tell him. We weren't married yet, and I was worried that this may be a deal breaker. I was working at the bank, and I made good friends there. I decided to tell my two best friends, Kimberly and Alysia, and a few other family members what was happening, but not Brian. When I finally did come clean, he just looked at me with so much love and said, "you should have told me earlier." He wasn't in the relationship for money. He loved me and he trusted that I would find a way out, and in the meantime, he wanted to help me in any way he could. He hadn't always made the best financial choices and was working through his own stuff. But he was a good man, and he was not going to let me just go down-hill without a fight. It became our fight. He knew he could help me more if we had one mortgage, and he was right, but because his mother lived there, it was not ideal. Let me correct that last sentence. It was not right in God's eyes, and it was bad for our relationship as a couple.

Moving in was hard on his mother because she had been the woman of the house since his divorce. His mother was not the only upset parent. My momma did not approve for one minute of the idea of me living with a man and his mother. She often told me, "If the milk is free, he's not going to buy the cow." Before I moved in, I asked him, "what changes can I make?" He said do whatever you want just leave Bricen's room as is. He didn't want anything to change for his son as he adjusted to me being there.

Brian lived like a real bachelor. He may not wash for weeks; he would just buy new clothes. There was no wall décor or whatnots on the counters. I'm not OCD but I do like to have order throughout my house. So, I decided to start with the kitchen. I spent a day organizing cabinets, putting in shelf liners, and changing the directions of the silverware. You name it, I did it. Well, these changes did not sit well with his mother. She was thinking who does this woman think she is? HA! As I think about it today, it was too much too soon. I guess I could have waited a couple of months. But again, he said go for it.

Over the next week, I went from room to room and bathroom to bathroom, except hers and Bricen's, making major décor changes. Because of my changes it started getting uncomfortable in the house. Brian's mother would be slamming kitchen cabinets at 4 a.m. saying I had thrown out something of hers. I'd go down and locate where I had moved it. That was the rule. Don't throw anything out, just organize. But that rule was not approved by Miss Cole. Although we tried to make it work, things did not go well, and I ended up moving out of Brian's home and moving in with a friend and her mother. I quickly learned what my mother told me and my sisters, "only one woman to a household."

We were only separated for three months, because Brian and I both knew we were better together than apart. I moved back in with Brian, and our mothers were not happy and rightfully so now that I look at it from their eyes.

The next few months were trying on us. Not only was Miss Cole no longer speaking to me, but she also stopped speaking to Brian. She would always make sure Bricen was taken care of and I made sure to stay out of her way. She wanted to dress and feed him. They also went outside daily to play. She was an awesome grandmother to Bricen.

One day Bricen asked his grandmother to make him something to eat, and I heard her say, "ask Earica." I was shocked! Something wasn't right. The next few days, we noticed she barely came out of her room, and she wasn't eating much. Brian went to check on her and she said she had been having severe lower back pains for the last few weeks. I gave him my heating pad for her, and he took her some medication. After a few more days, he encouraged her to make a doctor's appointment. She scheduled the appointment, but Brian had to work. He asked me to take her and with a bit of hesitation, I agreed. He looked me in my eyes and said, "When you go to this appointment, act like my mother is your mother. Ask all the questions you would for your mom. Please do this for me." I could see the concern in his eyes and hear it in his voice. I was concerned too, and I agreed with love.

The morning of the appointment, I waited downstairs for Miss Cole. I called up to her to see if she was ready. She said, "I need your help." She invited me into her room. I knew something was wrong! In two years, I had never been allowed to come near her bedroom! I opened the door and saw her struggling to put her pants on. I helped put them on and walked her down the steps. She was in so much pain! When we got to the doctor's office, I had to fill out her paperwork, after I went back into the examination room with her. The doctor was worried and wanted to run more test. He asked us to come back for more test in three days and I knew I could take off to be there. We left the appointment, and I took her to one of her favorite restaurants, Waffle House. But she didn't want to go in, so I ordered for us to take home. When we got home, she didn't want to eat so I took her upstairs to her room to rest. Later, when Brian got home and we talked, I could tell he was really worried about his mother.

That night, we heard her moaning and weeping all night. We decided to take her to the emergency room. As they were checking her in, Brian needed to leave for work. I stayed and I was going to head to work a little later. Luckily, Bricen was with his other grandmother. When the ER doctor examined her, he said he needed to speak to her primary care physician that she had seen the day before. But we had to wait until the office opened. I waited by Miss Cole's bed; she was in so much pain. I stepped outside and called my mother and asked her to pray for her. A few hours later, a nurse came in and said they had spoken to her doctor, and she needed to be admitted and he would be in before lunch. So, I called my job and told them I wouldn't be coming in. They gave Miss Cole some medicine to help her rest. The doctor was scheduled to see her around noon, so Brian took the rest of the day off to come and speak with the doctor. Shortly before Brian arrived, the doctor came into her room. He had some small talk with Miss Cole then asked to speak with me privately. We walked in the hallway, and he told me she had stage four pancreatic cancer. My heart dropped! I couldn't do this! How would I tell Brian or Miss Cole the news? Brian called me and said he was parking. I told him the doctor was here and needed to speak with him. The doctor said he was running to check on another patient and he would be right back. Moments after he walked away, Brian came off the elevator. I couldn't go back in that room without him. I tried to get him to wait for the doctor, but he insisted I tell him what was going on, so I did. He was devastated! He walked away and said he needed a few minutes alone. After about ten minutes, I went looking for him. He was in a hallway on the phone with one of his brothers. We just held each other and didn't say much. He had to figure out how to tell his mom.

Over the next few weeks. Brian and I both forgot about our problems and tried to bring his mother a sense of safety and good health while she was home. Recovery was not in God's plan, and Miss Cole passed in March 2011. Brian and his family were so heartbroken, and I was too. I am grateful for the time I had with her. I am grateful that God gave us time to heal our broken relationship. I am grateful for the fine son she raised. My time with her ran out, but she left behind a wonderful man to love me as much as I love him. Miss Cole left behind the man who taught me that YES… I could love again! Her last words to me were to take care of Brian and Bricen. Well, I hope Miss Cole is smiling. I've tried and I feel I did what she asked me to do for them. She would also be proud to know how much they love and take care of me.

A couple of months after we loss Miss Cole, Brian proposed. We both wanted a small wedding with our closest family and friends. It was so refreshing, we spent quality time with those who spent the last few years rooting for our love. While writing this book, we celebrated our 11th anniversary. We took a couple of international trips to celebrate. On our trip to Jamaica, the silliest but most profound thing popped into my head when Brian was out of the room. His phone was on the dresser, and I looked at it and smiled. When I was married before, any and every time Joe laid his phone down, I grabbed it the moment he was not looking. Looking for something that I already knew the answer to. Those days are so far behind me. I am so grateful!

Yes…yes. yes. Brian and I have had some bumps in the road throughout our relationship. We are both Aries, so we are both equally stubborn and we both believe we are right even when we are wrong. There was one vacation early in our relationship when we slept with the light on because we both refused to get up and turn it off. Stubborn us thought the other person was responsible for turning it on. Crazy right? That's something small and funny but it is not all fun and games. We've had to work through some trying times in our relationship but the difference this time is it's about US. It's never about a third party involved in our relationship. It's about the two of us adjusting our behaviors to work through our problems. Because we recognize the value, we add to each other. We also love ourselves. When you love who you are as a person, then you know how to show love to your partner, and you also know how to get your partner to love you. Yes, you can love again - but first you must love you!

CHAPTER 8

YOU ARE NOT HIS MOM

Not only did Miss Cole leave behind a wonderful son, but she also left a wonderful grandson who became my baby. I often hear my friends say that being a mother brought them the most joy, but it is their hardest job. They do not mean that in a negative way, but I know it is true. I did not give birth to Bricen, but he has been in my life since he was two years old. Being his stepmother is the hardest job I ever had, yet it brings me so much joy. Not because he is a difficult child, but the role of becoming a mother has been difficult.

I also listened, and still listen, to others talk about their stepchildren sometimes, and I am thinking "what a nightmare!" It is also a reminder of the relationship Shay not only had with Momma, but with Daddy too! I was not going to relive that with Bricen. Never! I needed him to love and respect me as a parent. But most importantly, I needed him to know that I loved and cherished him as a son. One thing I've learned is that when a child is acting out, it's probably because the adults involved are not united to make sure the child is healthy and happy. I didn't learn this from a book. I learned it firsthand watching my parents and Shay's mother. The environment looks and feels different, and they are struggling with accepting their new reality when the parents are divided.

Brian and his ex-wife do not have a bad relationship, and that has made my relationship with Bricen easier. They have an agreement that is cut and dry. They do not argue or treat each other poorly, and it's a breath of fresh air. When Bricen is with us, that's it… he is with us. When he is with his mother, he is with her. They truly parent together as adults and put his needs before their own, but there is not a lot of communicating. They trust and know that each one will always do what's right for their son.

I am a very vocal and opinionated person, so in the beginning, I always wanted to share my input with Brian and even his mother. I would press Brian to ask this and that, and he would push back reminding me that their methods worked for them, and I must respect their decisions. That was hard! Especially the first couple of years. We had to get professional counseling, and I had to trust that just because I saw several unhealthy step parenting situations, doesn't mean that they all end up that way. Getting counseling was a big move for us.

In the beginning, I really had to learn what my role was and trust me when I say it took time. When things didn't go the way I thought they should go, I withdrew. I would tell Brian; I was not Bricen's babysitter and would even leave the house and go to my mom's a few days to try and prove my point. But that wasn't the right way to handle that situation and my mother would quickly let me know that was wrong. What I was doing unknowingly was showing Bricen that I could and would leave whenever things got tough. I had to mature as co-parent.

I give Brian and his ex-wife credit for dissolving an unhealthy relationship as a couple but continuing to co-exist and raise their son. It has made it easy for me to have a good relationship with her when we do encounter each other. It is hard to convince a child that you love him or her, if you are talking poorly to his mother or father or treating them poorly. No one could talk bad to Momma and have a relationship with me.

What I did not let soak in when I was dating Brian was the fact that that there were four people raising Bricen. Brian, Bricen's mother, and his two grandmothers were all parenting him. After Ms. Cole died, I still didn't wrap my brain around the fact that marrying Brian meant I was number four as it related to his son. I thought being Brian's wife meant I would be raising Bricen with him and his ex-wife. None of that was true in the beginning.

Brian's mother was close to Bricen and the mother figure in the house. She adored Bricen, so there was really no place for me in that house or in the relationship. They did not need me to do anything for him, and it made me feel left out. Bricen's mother lived out of town, but her mother was in his life daily. She played the role of his mother too, and she took that role very seriously. She also worked at Bricen's elementary school, so she saw him daily, and had built relationships with the teachers and staff. There was no room for me, not even in his educational process. That made me uncomfortable. Attending events at school was not pleasant. I felt like the third wheel. I didn't ask questions because I didn't want to overstep. I never knew what to say or when my opinions of how his education should go were too much.

Remember, I came from a household where education was the priority. Games and toys were rewards for hard work. But Brian wanted Bricen to have more of a balance childhood. His dad was absent most of his childhood, so he was determined to have a close relationship with Bricen. They were like best friends. Most parents would just send their kids outside to play with a timestamp - but not Brian. He never allowed him to be outside without him or his mother. Most times, he would be outside with him running and playing with the kids. Like most parents, he wanted him to have the things that he never had.

105

So, we constantly bumped heads regarding school, until I made the decision to not make it an issue in our marriage. I only gave my opinion when asked.

Brian worked in retail and would leave the house most days when Bricen and I were asleep. So, I was responsible for getting Bricen's dressed, fixing breakfast, pack his lunch, and take him to his grandmothers who took him to school. There would be days when I came home from work that Bricen would have on something different from what he wore that morning. I would question Brian about it and his response was such a man's response, "who cares? He's dressed." Well, that didn't sit well with me. Bricen would even tell me not to cook because his grandmother was making him grits. After a few more of those instances, I decided to send Bricen to his grandmother in his pajamas and with an empty lunch box. Petty, right? Yep! I felt like it was a slap in my face when his lunch was changed, or clothes were changed. Again, I felt like the babysitter. Brian ironed Bricen's school uniform every morning, so it wasn't even clothes that I picked out. They were picked out by Brian, and it annoyed me that he wouldn't say anything. His response was always, "I just want peace." My response was that I was the only peace he should be worried about! Even with all the adult stuff going on behind the scenes, I still had a good relationship with Bricen from day one. I was not going to blame him for what the adults could not figure out. I helped him in any way I could, even when the adults did not want me to. My friends had children, so he really enjoyed going with me to birthday parties and various outings. We did fun things, and our bond was strong. So strong, that the instincts of motherhood kicked in when he needed me. He was, and is, the perfect son. There's no way you can't love a child with his personality and character.

Sometimes, it takes something bad to happen to correct things that we refuse to change on our own. That is what happened with Bricen. A few months after his mother corrected me on what he should call me (I will tell you more about that later), I noticed Bricen was not really himself. It had nothing to do with me; he was just not feeling well. He was not talking or eating much. A few days went by, and it was really bothering me. His mother was living in Birmingham, and she and Brian brushed it off as a cold. It was not that they were unconcerned, it was the fact they had all been raising him and they just thought I was a little over the top because Bricen was not feeling well. I was not buying that "it-is-a-cold" theory. I took a few days off from work to stay home with him. Remember, I'd been living with this child for almost two years now and had seen him interact and move about as an active child every single day. My gut told me that he was sick, and all their "I am not his mother" rules were about to go out the window. I did not care what they said or who would get mad. I called his dad and said, "Look, where is Bricen's insurance information? I want to take him to the hospital." He said, "Don't worry" and that Bricen would be okay, but he was not okay. I called his Bricen's grandmother, and she laughed it off for a minute because she assumed I was wrong since I didn't have children of my own. At least that's how it felt at that time. I remember her say, "poor thing" referring to me. She told me to make him some toast, and I could bring him to her. I was driving to the hospital. I called my mom, and she said I would need Brian to go to the hospital because Bricen was a minor. I was so frustrated! Once again, Momma was there to guide me. She didn't want me to repeat the mistakes that were made with Shay. She wanted me to be the stepmother to Bricen that she had tried to be to my sister.

Momma told me to just calm down and talk to Brian when he got home. He loves Bricen and he will do what's best. By the time Brian got home from work, Bricen was really fading. I watched him holding Bricen and he was patting him on the back. He said his grandmother thought it may be gas. I was infuriated! But I had to be calm. His temperature was high, and he was no longer throwing up because he was dehydrated. He was just gagging as if he needed to throw up. He had a bad night, and his temperature was getting higher. Brian realized this was out of hand, and we rushed him to the local hospital.

When we got to the hospital, I could tell Brian was worried. I still get tears in my eyes when I think about the words that came out of the doctor's mouth. "One of your son's lungs has collapsed, and the other one will too. He has pneumonia. We cannot treat him here, and he must be taken to the children's medical hospital immediately." They prepared him for transfer and Brian jumped in the ambulance with Bricen, and I followed them in Brian's truck as Brian alerted Bricen's mother and grandmother. I called my family, and we all went into prayer immediately.

His condition was listed as critical, and they took him to ICU. My heart dropped. I watched Brian melting in the waiting room as Bricen's mother and grandmother arrived. When the doctor came out, he explained what was happening. Then he said, "Only three people can be with him." I knew that meant I would not see Bricen. I stood there and watched his parents and grandmother disappear into his room. Once again, I felt left out of the equation. I walked to the waiting area and cried. But I had to throw my foolish pride away. I needed to focus on what was happening on the other side of that door. I wanted my baby to live.

They needed to put a needle in his arm for the IV and Bricen did not like needles, in fact he hated them. Brian came and got me. He said, "You will have to be in here for them to put this IV in his arm." Bricen always needed to be my superhero, so he wasn't going to let me see him scared. We had that type of connection. He looked in my eyes and I told him it was going to be easy. I told him I get these needles when I go to the doctor for my sickle cell treatments. He was much stronger than me.

After a month in the hospital, Bricen recovered, thank God, and one of the happiest days of my life was when he came home. I learned one of the greatest lessons of my life as the sun came up that morning and his condition improved. I learned that being a mother is being there for a child in need. I was able to work from home and spend most days at the hospital. We would all take shifts to nurse him back to good health, and he became a normal, playful, little boy again.

When Bricen came home from the hospital, he out of the blue started calling me Mom every now and then. I must admit I was happy because I loved him like he was my son. I will always see him as my son. A few months after he started calling me Mom, we went to pick Bricen up from his grandmother's house after church one Sunday. His mother was in town, and he stayed the weekend with her. When we arrived, she followed us outside in the garage while Bricen went to grab his bag. She walked up to me and spoke like we always do. Without being mean she said, "Hey, can I talk to you two?" I could tell she was concerned, so we stopped in the garage. "I don't want Bricen calling Earica, Mom. I'm his mother." She explained a story that Bricen was sharing with her family, and he said, "my mom said…" She responded she didn't say that, and he said, "my mom Earica." Brian walked off. I know what he was thinking. He knows his wife! But honestly, first, I was shocked. Secondly, I was proud of my response. I said, I understood and explained that's not something that I had asked nor required. Now Brian almost passed out because he thought he was getting ready to witness a world war! But no! We were two grown women having an adult conversation. I've got to be honest. I remember my daddy on his death bed saying, "I'm your papa, and I'm your only papa." Those words changed me. Some may disagree, but at that moment, I realized that although I adore Bricen, he's not my biological child and there are boundaries. Difficult but it's a reality. He has a mother, and there's a bond they share that I can't and shouldn't try to replace. I share a bond with Bricen that is unshakeable, and so is our love. After our encounter, we went home and back to our normal life as he started calling me Earica again. I'm sure she had a conversation with Bricen, but it changed nothing between us, and I am so grateful for that.

In all honestly, I did not care what he called me after almost losing him. I still do not care. My prayer was just to hear his little voice again when he was sick. God answered that prayer! If I did not understand my love for him, it was made clear after that night in the hospital. I understood that night that all your children will not be your biological children. God will send you children to love and protect. He sent me Bricen. He sent me my son in every way that counts!

I will never forget his grandmother apologizing to me for any misunderstandings we had in the past. She kept repeating, "You saved his life," as she hugged me tightly! That moment changed our relationship. I felt she truly recognized I loved her grandson. She saw me for the first time. But I did not save his life. That was God! God helped me to see what others could not see. That is what I want you to know and understand if you are a stepparent. Do what is best for the child, even when you are uncomfortable. All I could think about was the fact that God put it on my heart that this poor child was in trouble.

Over eleven years have gone by since that night. Bricen graduated from high school while I was writing this book. I thought about so many things as he walked across that stage. I was reminded of his little laughter at birthday parties. I thought about how we almost lost him all those years ago, and God gave him back to us as a healthier child. After graduation, we had a big party for him. My family, his mother, stepfather, Brian, and I gathered with all the people who loved Bricen. A few days later, I overheard him talking to my God parents. "That was the best day of my life," he said with pride as he chatted about his party. But on that day, on graduation day, I kept thinking that is my baby! No matter what he calls me, that is my son! Step parenting may not always be easy, but for me, it has always been worth it. Once I realized he was not my stepson but my bonus son. God gave me another heart and soul to love. Bricen may not have grown inside my belly, but he sure grew inside my heart!

CHAPTER 9

GIRL DAD

I am a huge Kobe Bryant fan! When he passed, I was heartbroken like millions of people were around the world. It is one of those moments that you remember where you were and what you were doing when you heard the news. I was in my bedroom watching television, when the first report came across the news. That is where I stayed all day. I was numb as fake reports began to spread on social media, and then the horrible truth that none of us wanted to hear started to come to us via every news outlet in the world. I do not mean only local and United States news outlets, I mean the entire world! He was that well known... an international superstar. Now he was gone. Kobe and eight beautiful people were gone including his precious daughter. I was sad for all the lives lost that day. As for Kobe, I felt like I had lost a cousin. His unmatched skills in basketball and his transition to a great businessman and family man made him an icon that I admired heavily.

I could not stop watching old clips of Kobe playing basketball and looking at pictures of him online. The pictures that stood out to me were the pictures of him with his wife and children. I noticed that even before his retirement, social media was filled with pictures of Kobe Bryant the father and husband. I am sure I had seen all the pictures before, but they looked different now. All I could think about was the lives left behind to grieve. During my grief, something happened that gave me, and I think a lot of other people, peace. News anchors around the world were still talking about Kobe when they aired an interview of him talking about his children. His girls! He said his friends teased him about not having a son. He said, "That does not bother me. I am a girl dad." My heart melted when I heard those words. Social media lit up with the term, "Girl Dad." As strange as it sounds, it made me feel better. When I think about him now, I think about him being a "girl dad" before I think about basketball.

Yes, he was a star! A superstar! But those words told us that his greatest love was his family! His girls! I tear up thinking about that moment. I was hurting for Vanessa and their three beautiful girls, but I found joy in two little words. GIRL DAD! I found joy because I knew what that meant. My dad was a "girl dad." Not only to me and Shay, but to Kathy and all his goddaughters too.

There was nothing my Daddy would not do for us. Even though he has been gone for over 22 years, he is still the person that has the most influence over me. I think about what he would do whenever I am unsure about situations in my personal and business life. I miss my dad, but I somehow feel like he never really left me. During the most important or difficult situations in my life, I can feel his presence. I can even hear his voice.

Yes, I was born with sickle cell, but not diagnosed properly until I was around five years old. Even before I was diagnosed, I was in and out of hospitals and doctors' offices all the time. I missed school a lot and cried whenever I was in pain. Momma and daddy cradled me and covered my face with kisses to help me make it through each crisis. Everything changed when I was around nine years old. My health was declining, and I had been having serious sickle crises constantly. One crisis was so severe that I was rushed to the hospital. The doctors were really concerned because my platelet counts were off. They wanted to give me a blood transfusion, but my parents wanted to wait to see how I did on the medication. My parents did not leave my side. My sisters, Trinnett and Trina, also took turns staying in my room. My cousin Rico was in another room on another floor because of his recent crisis, and he would visit me in his wheelchair. He wasn't on the kids' floor because he was older. I do not remember everything that happened in the hospital, but I remember what happened when I came home.

My mom's brother, Uncle Joseph, asked my parents to check me out of the hospital and he invited us to his church in Tallahassee, Florida on the Hill. He told Momma to bring me there for his revival. They were having two evangelists in town, and he wanted them to physically pray for me. Now Daddy didn't go but he agreed with mom taking me. He wasn't attending church at that time, but he trusted and loved Uncle Joseph. He knew that he would always care for me as his own child. Momma packed our bags, took me out of the hospital and we were off to the revival. During the first couple of days at the revival, I laid on the back pew still in pain. I would eat a little bit, but mostly, they gave me fluids and Momma would rub my body while she prayed. The last day of revival was a Saturday morning. When it was time for people to go to the alter to pray, my uncle motioned for Momma to bring me down to him. You know that saying; leave your prayers at the altar. Momma laid me down on a pew at the altar. The evangelists and other church folks gathered around me and prayed. I mean really prayed. I remember passing out and when I came to, the pain was gone! The church folks, including my mother, started shouting and praising God. Even I, as a 10-year-old, started praising God. I didn't know what happened, but I knew that my life was forever changed.

I have no idea what Momma told Daddy when we went back to Jacksonville. I don't know if she gave him the details. I also did not know why he did not go with us to revival until years later. He told me, while I was in the hospital, he went to God in prayer. He asked God for a miracle. He asked God to heal me and end my suffering. That is exactly what God did. Dad also promised God that he would give his life to Him if he would just heal his baby girl. He promised that he would attend church and live the life of a Christian man. That is also exactly what my late father did.

A few months after going to revival, Daddy had his own moment at the altar. Without warning us, he attended church with us one Sunday. I was shocked! My dad never went to church. At the end of the service, he got up and walked to the front of the church. In true Jerome Alexander style, he did it his way. He asked for the microphone. That is still so funny to me, but what he said was not funny in the least. He turned his life over to God, and that is the way he lived out his days. He did that for me, but it was also his road to healing so many broken things in his own life. He started going to church with us every Sunday and throughout the week, and he just became a better man.

Can you believe that I slept with my parents until I was thirteen? I know! Crazy right? Yes, I slept in their bed, and most of the time, I slept across the top of their heads. That's where I felt most comfortable. I also sucked my thumb until age thirteen, and my dad didn't allow anyone to try and stop me. Honestly, I think that was his way of keeping me a little girl. We would watch *Sanford and Son* every night before I went to bed. Most times, I never wanted to spend the night at others' houses because I preferred to sleep with my parents. When I did, I would sneak away and call my daddy to come get me.

Although my dad was a great father and provider, he wasn't a great husband. Well at least not in my eyes. Wow! I can't believe I just wrote that, but it's true. I never saw my dad show my momma public affection. There were never surprises of flowers or secret getaways. We would have family gatherings all the time, but I never saw my dad give Momma undivided attention. I also remember my dad speaking to Momma like she was a child in front of others. One time he told her to shut up when there were several people around. She was giving her opinion about something. I could tell she was humiliated. Shay and I were so angry at him that I cried! I knew as a teenager I didn't want the kind of marriage they had. No one, and I mean no one, has permission to holler at me like a child. If you want to quickly lose my attention in a conversation, raise your voice. I no longer hear what you're saying because now I'm enraged at your tone. I recognize it's a trigger for me because of how my dad used to talk to my mother.

On Valentine's Day and Mother's Day, her girls would try to surprise her. I even told my dad he needed to be a better husband to Momma. His reply was always, "I take care of her." For Mother's Day if we asked him to get Momma a gift, he said, "She ain't my mother." But that wasn't enough. I knew Momma wanted romance, but she never said anything. She just accepted who he was and what their marriage had become. She fell into the settling trap. I saw that amongst a lot of women in her generation. It appeared because their husbands were great providers, the wives allowed their spouses to talk to them in a disrespectful manner. No sir! Not me! If you want respect then you better give it, buddy! My dad was quick to always holler the scripture in the Bible that wives needed to submit to their husbands. Unfortunately, he forgot the verse in the bible about the husbands loving their wives like Christ loved the church. But that was always a great debate between him and Shay.

So, when Marvin, my stepdad, came into Momma's life five years after my dad died, although I was hesitant, I loved how he loved Momma. She remained his girlfriend throughout their marriage. I had never seen Momma smile or laugh the way she did with him. That helped me accept him. No, he wasn't my daddy, and as far as I was concerned, he would never be "my papa," but clearly, he wanted nothing more than to make Momma happy, and that was enough for me.

Over the years, I have kept the lessons from my daddy close to my heart as I moved around in the world. The good and the bad. Throughout his careers, he was a voice for his African American colleagues. He wanted them to be treated fairly and be given the same opportunities that others had. He worked hard and climbed the corporate ladder. He gave his life to Christ and served in his church as an elder. He was a great father and provider for his family. He left me with a passion for his favorite football team, the Dallas Cowboys. But most importantly, he taught me to never sell myself short, and never accept failure. I was always more than enough. A loss is just a lesson on how to win the next time.

CHAPTER 10

I'M NOT YOUR AACE

I thank God every day for my parent's wisdom. I needed everything they taught me when I joined Corporate America. There were times I know I did exactly what my dad would have done when I had to make decisions. There are also times I know I did just the opposite of what Daddy would have done. One incident, at my place of employment in Atlanta, stands out more than all the others. I think a lot about the situation that I am about to share with you. I think it would have disappointed my Daddy to know I handled myself in this matter. Not only would it have disappointed him, I am disappointed when I think about my response, but I know it will *never* happen again.

I think about numerous incidents that happened in my career when I was younger, that would never happen now. When I reached 40 years old, I did a lot of reflecting on my life. I was forced to look at my entire life as I wrote this book because I wanted to be totally transparent with my readers. I found myself taking inventory of all the people in my life, places I have been and most of all, the experiences I had. I feel proud of my accomplishments and try not to beat myself up too much about areas that some may see as failures.

I think about things that I could have done to make a difference in someone's life. Most of those thoughts go back to my time in Corporate America. I do not feel I failed me. I just know I could have done more for others. When I say others, I mean other minorities, black women. Yes, that is it! I said it aloud. I wish I had done more for black women.

When I say more, I mean I had opportunities that some of them did not have. Some of my job titles and salaries came with an unwritten responsibility of ensuring the success of the organization. But I always wanted my staff to be treated fairly and sometimes those two objectives were not aligned. There were times that I feel I should have served the employee vs. serving the organization. My Daddy understood that very well. He was not at Southern Bell to just earn a paycheck; he was making a real difference. Yes, he was very vocal, and I mean *vocal*, but that was his way. If he saw someone doing something wrong, on or off the job, you were going to hear from Jerome! I promise you; his colleagues were happy when he retired! Not because he was not doing a great job, but because he was in their face if he saw any sign of prejudice against minorities.

After his early retirement, he became an investigator for the Equal Employment Opportunity Commission (EEOC). My dad worked tirelessly, trying to make sure justice was served in the workplace for everyone. I, on the other hand, cannot say I did everything I could have done. Regardless of skin color, I was going to hire the person who was most qualified for the position, and I mentored them in the areas where I saw weakness. Giving people opportunities is a wonderful feeling, but it is not a good feeling when I think back to not standing up for people when I knew with everything in me that they were treated unfairly. I learned from my father at an early age what black leadership looked like. I learned what it sounded like, and the mere presence of black excellence when we walked in the room.

Throughout my career, I had black and white professional mentors. But there was clearly a difference in their approaches. My minority mentors were very diplomatic. They were cautious with their words and their tone of voice. They would often remind me that the tone was so important as it would be perceived as anger from a black leader. On the other hand, my white mentors were very direct. They were no-nonsense and no one ever questioned their tone. You just did what they said with no questions asked.

Because I knew what it looked like, I should have known what to do when I saw doors being closed for people around me.

Closed not because they were not doing a good job, but because they were not the status quo for the role. Closed because they did not look the way other white managers thought they should look, or dress. It was very subtle remarks that were made in my presence. Questions that were asked. Long pauses after my response. Then, of course the decisions that went a different way that couldn't be explained.

Working in the banking industry was like no job I had ever worked in before, due to all the security protocols, rules, and regulations. The people in power let you know that this is not the place you can come to get a do-over. You cannot make mistakes with other people's money. That is rule number one. I consider myself a fast learner, and I account that to my many promotions, which led me to become an executive.

While I was the Director of Training for an organization, the craziest thing ever happened to me, and it was about black women and our hair. That is right, hair! I was always the woman changing her hair style daily, but I was always "conservative." Simple and straight or pulled into a bun. Translate that to I did not embrace my natural hair. I dared not wear braids, an afro or anything that spelled black woman, loud and clear. Even my accessories were very simple and classic. My nails were French manicured or a neutral color.

Because I was in management, my office was in the corporate building. One day, a new employee that was hired came by for a training session. She was the epitome of young, gifted, and black. She also wore her beautiful blackness in a way I did not. Her hair! When I, along with the COO, interviewed her, she had her hair straightened. But when she started the job, her hair was full, and she often wore it in an afro. She was doing an excellent job, so I had no idea what was happening when the COO came by my office and spoke.

COO: "Earica, I want to talk to you about the new girl."

Me: "New girl? Who are you talking about?"

COO: "The lady who just walked in with the big hair."

Me: "That is X. We just hired her."

COO: "Really, she looks different. Her hair was not like that in the interview. Can you talk to her? I want her hair to look like yours."

I was shocked, and initially speechless. How do I respond so that I don't get fired? So, I slowly said, "Well, black women choose to wear their hair natural or straight. I choose straight, but clearly, she chooses natural. She doesn't appear to have a relaxer." This jackass had the nerve to say to me, "what about those wig thingies you all wear?" My only response was, "Let me see how to address it." He then said, "Thank you, can you imagine standing behind her in a line?" He chuckled and I gave a fake smile. I do not remember how the conversation ended. There I was explaining a sister's blackness to a white man. There I was telling him I had a relaxer, so my hair was straight just the way he liked it, and her hair was not. She was wearing the crown of my ancestors and she did not have to explain that to him or to me. He kept calling me his "AACE." I finally asked what that meant. He said I was his African American Cultural Expert. Of course, he did not know what I was thinking. He walked out of my office, and I was floored! I was so hot and had no clue of how to handle it.

If there was a moment in my life that I was supposed to remember who my daddy was, it was that day. No one at Southern Bell could have said that to Daddy, because he would have raised the water out of the Red Sea. He was that guy! I did not have to take the roof off the way Daddy would have, but I was supposed to correct our COO. You are probably wondering why I didn't. I did not for the same reason black people have kept their mouths closed for four hundred years. The same reason that women and homosexuals who were mistreated and looked over for positions for which they were qualified. FEAR! Of course, I was not afraid of being beaten like my enslaved ancestors. There is no comparison, but I was afraid of him not thinking I was his golden girl anymore. I was afraid of him not giving me a promotion or a raise. He was next in line to become the company's President, and I thought he would continue to promote me - so I fell silent when he marched into my office talking about freaking hair! Yep, I'm ashamed but never again! There were other times when he said things that made me question his bigotry. He would ask if someone was gay or if they were pregnant before offering a position. But it was after that moment, which was one of several, that I decided to have a voice in the community. I would no longer be quiet about injustices regardless of the organization, its' views, or the leader's personal opinions. This was a defining moment for me.

Our ancestors feared separation from their family. That's what happened to my grandfather after standing up for himself. After slavery, they feared starving to death if they left the plantation, even though they were free. That cycle just continued from one generation to another. Afraid to be killed! Afraid to lose their children. Afraid to be kicked out of their house if they voted! I was afraid I would not make it to the top! For that, I am ashamed! For that, I ask God to help me to never live in fear for myself or my people! I made the decision to be a voice for those who were voiceless. I would use my positions to give qualified people the opportunity to succeed and grow in every way I could.

I pulled myself together after he left my office. Everything my parents ever taught me came back. I got up and went to Human Resources to report him. One of my friends was a HR rep, and she was an African American. She was stunned! She told me how to handle the situation. The HR Vice President was a white woman, and I reported directly to her. She was genuinely mortified when I told her what happened. She said she would talk to him, and she did. He later apologized for his comments, but of course our relationship was never the same. Now check this out. Two years later, he was fired for inappropriate relationships with several women in the office as he transitioned to the role of CEO. One of the women was a black woman! That broke my heart! Let's be clear, I was broken hearted for all the women he had used for his pleasure. We are not your pleasure! We are queens, for ourselves, nobody else!

I cannot change what happened before I was born, but I can make a difference now. Today, my response would be different if anyone, I mean anyone, approached me with such foolishness. I would immediately say, "Excuse me but I am uncomfortable with this conversation. I know you do not understand our culture or black hair, but I am happy to discuss it with you as a proud black woman." It took me years to wear braids or various ethnic hairstyles because I witnessed the discrimination firsthand! Now, I love wearing protective styles for my beautiful crown and I dare anyone to ask me to straighten my hair to make *them* comfortable.

I know that is the right response to anyone trying to make people of color feel less-than based on how they think we should look. We cannot exist in a world looking over our shoulders daily. We cannot exist being afraid to say the wrong thing, even when we know there is injustice. Our purpose is so much more than that.

I am telling this story for all the little girls and women who live in fear of something or someone. Don't be afraid of who you are. Remember whose you are! Do not be afraid of your culture. It is a culture that has the blood, sweat and tears of your ancestors tied into the fabric of our fancy business suits. The leadership role that you have, was not only because you worked your way to the top. You are there because a lot of people of paved the way. If you are in Corporate America today… good for you! Make the best out of your time there. Do what you need to do and enjoy your career! Save your money now, so that you can have options later. Whatever you do, keep your dignity, and stand up when it is time to stand up!

CHAPTER 11

MY ILLNESS DOESN'T DEFINE ME

We face so many fears in our lifetime. I was barely in school when I was faced with the fear of sickle cell anemia. Only God had the power to give me the strength to say, "NO," I don't want to be scared every day of my life. Do you want to know what living with sickle cell anemia taught me? It taught me to not let sickle cell anemia live with me. Let me explain! Before I even knew what sickle cell anemia meant, I knew I could not do things that other kids could do. Once I was diagnosed, I felt like I had a laundry list of "things not to do." It was not easy to understand as a child.

When I was old enough to really understand what was happening to my body, I also understood that I had control over my life. Two of the most important things that living with sickle cell has taught me, is the power of God and the protection of family. Yes, I was frustrated with the rules of what I could and could not do because of sickle cell, but I know my parents were just trying to protect me. They knew that their love and support are important because on the outside of your home, you do not know what is waiting for your children. Yes, I met many wonderful friends along the way, but consistent love for me started once I was at home. Once I walked out of that door, Mommy and Daddy could not protect me.

I was around six years old when we went on a trip to Atlanta to visit some of my parents' friends. They had a nice home with a huge swimming pool in their backyard. The adults were standing on the balcony that overlooked the pool while talking and playing cards, and Momma was chatting with some of her friends. I decided I would take a dive in the pool with the other kids. No swimming lessons, nothing! I just jumped in the pool. Honey, Daddy jumped off the balcony directly into the pool, like freaking Chadwick Boseman, and saved me. He pulled me to safety as Momma ran down the steps. I guess Momma said, "I am not getting my hair wet messing with that girl!" HA! Momma couldn't swim like my dad, so it was best that she didn't jump in after all.

Everybody gathered around the pool and looked at us. They looked at Daddy like... what the heck? Did you just jump off a balcony into a pool? My Daddy did not care! If I was in trouble, or anyone he loved, Daddy was taking a dive! He would do anything for his children. When I think back to that day, I realize he could have landed wrong and injured himself. He did not care! He was going to save his Sugar Foot!

At that point, my parents realized that that I would push the envelope. They realized that I was not going to let sickle cell control my life. I would not take no for an answer, so they quickly put me in swimming lessons. They knew I would be off somewhere, one day jumping in somebody's pool, and Daddy would not be there to save me. It was not just about swimming and loving the water. It was about me wanting to live my life. Live my life to the fullest and not as a sickle cell patient every day. Every introduction would start off with, "watch her closely, she has sickle cell."

I not only learned to swim, but I became a great swimmer. Yes, Momma and family members still get nervous when I get in the pool, but I am doing fine. The water brought me joy then and now. I love going to beaches when I'm traveling. When I became a teenager, I wanted to participate in more activities. I wanted to go places with my friends, and the answer was often "no" from my parents. I just could not stand the word 'no,' and I am still that way today. My parents made a compromise and would let me go places, but Trinnett, Trina or Kathy always had to go along. I felt like a little kid going out with my friends, with a babysitter following me around. I was not embarrassed because my friends knew what was going on. I just wanted my freedom. My sisters tagging along was just another reminder that I had sickle cell. I was like Miss Sophia in *The Color*

Purple. "There's going to be some changes around here." That is what I told myself every day.

One of my favorite things to do as a child, was go to the amusement park and get on the rides. Once again, my big sisters were always a few steps behind me. Kathy and Momma took me to a local fair, and I begged them to get on a rollercoaster. They were hesitant, but Momma said I could only get on if Kathy rode with me. Well, after a few sharp turns on that ride, Kathy and Momma knew something was wrong. Momma watched from below as Kathy was screaming, "stop the ride!" I began to panic, and they saw the fear in my eyes. Momma made them stop the ride, and when I got off, I cried, and we went home. A couple of days later, I had one of my worse sickle cell crises as a child. But I needed my family to understand that one incident didn't mean I wanted to be put in a cell and not allowed to do anything like other kids.

I went to my parents and told them I just did not want my siblings with me every day. I knew my condition, but I needed them to trust me. That was my get-out-of-jail card. That was it for me. No more babysitters. I started doing things on my own. Momma was terrified, but she knew I wanted to live, and she just had to trust God to take care of me.

For years, I never told people I had sickle cell. While attending school, if I got sick and needed days off, I would make up excuses. I never wanted pity! I didn't want to be treated differently, and if you tried to, there was a problem. When I went off to college, Momma was worried, but I did okay and my leaving FAMU had nothing to do with sickle cell anemia. She made Trina and Trinnett keep their eyes on me while there. She tried to have my uncle and aunt monitor me closely, but I was good at dodging them. Technology wasn't what it is now!

As time went on, I learned what to do and when to slow down if I felt my body was about to go into a crisis. I also learned that there is more to life than just surviving. I do not ever want to just survive! It is important to thrive, and that is what I do daily. Situations will alter your life. Sickle cell has altered my life, but it never stopped me from living it to the fullest. Yes, there are days that I must listen to my body and rest. But I'm not going to miss opportunities or experiences because of this illness.

My grandmother was the epitome of never stop living your best life. She was diagnosed with breast cancer and refused treatments. She was often told she would not live another year. Can I tell you she lived over twenty years with breast cancer and lived life to the absolute fullest? No, I wasn't accepting disability. I wasn't accepting not going to college. I wasn't accepting not being able to travel and create other experiences. Let me stop here and caution you to not do what my grandmother did.

For years different organizations asked me to be a spokesperson for Sickle Cell, but I said no. No, I wasn't ashamed, and I believe in the good work that they do. I've always struggled with that platform to say yes because I struggle with breathing life into my health situation daily. I feel like the more you talk about something, it becomes who you are. I am not sickle cell anemia! It does not define me.

My husband would get so upset with me when we first dated. I would drive myself to a nearby hospital or call rescue and then call him later once I started feeling better. The thought of him sitting next to me watching me in pain just didn't sit well with me. But his first experience with me being sick and not being able to run from him was in Mexico. We were on vacation, and I'm not sure if it was the altitude or if I was just dehydrated. I got sick about two days into our trip. I refused to go to the doctors, because I wasn't sure if the medical facilities there were knowledgeable of sickle cell treatments. We were told not to drink the water while there, but of course, that's what I needed to help flush my cells. He was searching around the resort property for bottles of purified water to get me through the next two days, before we left. I still remember the fear in his eyes as he watched me squeal in pain. We were boiling water in the coffee Keurig to create heating pads.

In all honesty, my doctors always tell me that I'm not a normal sickle cell patient. My crises are so far apart now that I can sometimes go years without pain. I do get regular tests ran, and I know when my body is telling me to rest and drink more fluids. I'll also get iron transfusions as needed. Laying on that church bench, in 1987 at the revival, changed my life. I know that God gave me a supernatural experience that I can't explain. But I'm so grateful to be alive! I know that there is work for me to do here, and I'm not going to waste it worrying about the next crisis or avoiding experiences to prevent a crisis. Live your life, people. Live to the fullest. Love hard, and for God's sake, when love finds you, embrace it with everything inside of you.

CHAPTER 12

MY SISTER'S KEEPER

I've had my share of loss throughout my life. But nothing is as hard as talking about losing my sister. Losing the one person in the world who had the same Jerome Alexander blood running in her veins. Losing, Shay. I know I talked about my sister earlier in this book, but I want to go deeper into why the words, "my sister's keeper," really matters.

People always say you cannot save other people, but I do wish I could have done more to help my sister. While writing this book, we celebrated and mourned what would have been her 50th birthday. That day was so hard for me. It was my hardest day since she left us. It was hard because I could not shake all the things she will never be able to do; all the things she will not be able to do with her children and her grandchildren. She will not grow old with me and our other sisters. She will not enjoy the golden years that I've watched Momma enjoy with her sisters. There will be no golden years for Shay.

I spent most of her birthday trying to understand what went wrong. I have replayed the call we received, telling us that Shay was gone, a thousand times. It is the call that no one wants to receive at 4:00 a.m. Brian's cellphone just kept ringing repeatedly. He was fast asleep, but it woke me up and I woke him to tell him to see what was going on. I thought it was one of his siblings, and I am so glad I did not answer his phone.

Brian answered, and I just heard him say, "yes. This is he. Oh' NO! Let me get my wife on the phone." He was clearly upset and shaken.

I took the phone and heard the man's voice.

"Are you Earica Cole?"

I remember saying "yes" as my life became a horror movie in one telephone call.

He said, "I was scrolling through Shay's phone, and she had Brian's number listed as Brother-in-Law." I assume they ran a quick background check on him and knew Shay was my sister. He asked me to verify Shay's birthday. After I did, he said the words, "I am so sorry to tell you this, but your sister has been murdered." That will stay in my head the rest of my life. The pain will stay in my heart the rest of my life. I screamed and Brian just grabbed me and held me. I had not really digested what he said, so my next words were, "did you arrest the killer? If not, I know who did it." I said that because Shay had shared with me how violent her previous relationship had become with her ex-husband. She had recently tried to work things out with him, so that was my natural response.

The next words out of the officer's mouth shattered me.

"Yes, we arrested her son. He confessed to the murder."

I was silent. When he finished talking, I was shaking. No way! How? Why? Am I dreaming? I kept saying, "Oh My God. What happened?" The man explained that he was the coroner and I needed to speak with the detective of the case. He asked how soon I could be in Atlanta. It was surreal, because I was scheduled to travel to Atlanta that day for a speaking engagement with my sisters. I told him I'd be there by noon. I asked did I have to identify her. I remember him saying, "no ma'am. That's not something I recommend you doing." I knew then it was bad. My sister died tragically, and I wasn't there! I hung up and screamed and cried. I had not cried like that since Daddy died. Brian was devastated, but he tried to console me. There was no comfort. There were no words to help me understand. When I pulled myself together, I did what I always do. I called Kathy. It was in the middle of the night, and I just could not call Shay's mother or my Momma first.

We cried together as sisters, and then we had to call Momma. No matter what had happened in the past, Momma loved Shay, and she was inconsolable. I had to tell her daughter. How was I supposed to do this? I asked Kathy what to say. Should I go there? Who would be there to console her? Kathy explained I needed to do it before someone else did. I started thinking about the media. Was this going to be on the news? I didn't know what to do, but I knew I had to be there for my niece.

The unfortunate distance in my relationship with Shay over the years meant, I missed a lot of my niece's and nephew's lives. They were both in my first wedding as little kids, but it was over 15 years before I saw them again. The last interaction I had with my niece was when I told her and her mother that I loved them less than two months ago. The only things she knew about me were the things her mother told her. How would she take this news from me?

Now, I had to contact Shay's mother. Unfortunately, their relationship was strained too. That was how it was with Shay. If she was done with you, it was hard to reconnect. But I knew her mother loved her and needed to know. I learned that the coroner was able to reach her as well. She and I were both in disbelief. But we both had one goal, and that was to make sure my niece was okay and protected. I thought about Daddy. He would have been crushed if he had lived long enough to hear the words, "Shay is dead."

Kathy talked to me, she told me that we needed to do a conference call with my sisters and tell them at the same time. That was the worst call of all. Their screams and cries out to God broke me. When we finally pulled ourselves together, I told them that I had to be the one to tell Shay's daughter. When I called her, she was living with a friend at the time. I knew she was in shock. She was clearly distraught and asked what she needed to do. She asked a few other questions and said, "Should I go to work tomorrow?" That is how traumatized she was. I told her to call in and explain what happened. Poor baby, she had just loss her mother and her brother. Just imagine that trauma. Imagine the pain! I told her I was leaving in a few hours to go to Atlanta, and I'd send for her to meet me there. Throughout the day, I just kept checking on her. I immediately felt I needed to look out for her.

When the sun came up, it was still so dark to me. The day was a blur. The days that followed were a blur too. I was scheduled to go to Atlanta on business, so I just kept those plans as my sisters made plans to meet me there. When my plane arrived, I just could not believe that I was in Atlanta to go to my sister's house, and she was no longer there. A couple of my girlfriends met me at the police station. They held me and we cried together. At that moment I was so thankful for my true friendships. They even came with me to meet the detective to learn what happened.

After meeting with the detectives, he told me that we were free to go to Shay's home and retrieve her items. He gave us a report to give a locksmith so they could open the door. I was not prepared for that moment. I assumed we would have a police officer meet us at her house and allow us to move everything out. That's not how it happens in real life. You are expected to get it done by any means necessary.

I called Momma and Kathy, and they were adamant for me not to go to that house alone. April and Trinnett were on the way, and I needed to wait. They both said I needed to eat something and drink some fluids. I knew they were worried about me having a crisis. I took their advice and went to try and get something eat with my friends. I was in a daze, but they both knew I needed to eat. I made a few calls to family members that needed to know, and my Uncle Joseph called to pray with me for strength. I wept uncontrollably and he begin to speak peace over me. It was at that moment that I knew everything would be on me. The arrangements, moving her personal items, notifying everyone. Making sure my niece was okay.

Making sure justice was served. I quickly pulled myself together.

Out of all my sisters, my two sisters that are very emotional were on the way. I knew I had to be there for them too. They loved Shay and unfortunately, their relationship had been strained too. I had never been to Shay's house, but I saw on social media that she had moved into a house several months prior to the tragedy. Yes, that's how she would often "share" things with us. We found out on Facebook. When it was announced, I immediately knew that she didn't personally own it because I knew what her financial situation was at that time. But I was thankful she had a place to stay and somewhere I thought she would be safe. I just messaged her and said, "I'm happy for you."

Rewind three years prior when Shay went through an ugly divorce and lost everything. I mean everything. My well educated, talented, and beautiful sister was in an abusive relationship and walked away from it with the clothes on her back. We had just reconnected a year prior after almost ten years of no contact. Of course, I did everything I could to help her. I was all she had. I refused to allow my sister to be homeless, so I made sure she had a place to stay. I had to get her out of some poor financial decisions, and I refused to judge

144

her. We've all had our low moments in life, and I knew she needed me. I was glad that my husband and I were in a place that we could help. She was getting on her feet, and I was so happy for her. She went to stay with Momma for a couple of months to figure out what she would do next. Momma's husband, Marvin, had passed, so Momma wanted the company, and she knew Shay needed us. Although she and mom hadn't spoken in years, Momma knew she needed her and wanted to make sure she was safe.

I was in the process of getting ready to move to Alabama for a new job. She came with me for a few weeks, while my husband stayed back in Atlanta until his job transfer was final. I tried to get her to move to Alabama so that we could be closer and work on our relationship. But Shay wanted to become a Georgia resident to take the Georgia bar. So, when I saw the house she posted on social media, I didn't care that it was rented. It just looked like security, and that is all that mattered to me. I was proud that my sister was turning her situation around. There were still so many unanswered questions about her life, but I never wanted to push. I was just happy that we were trying to spend more time together.

When we arrived at her house, I was horrified. The doors and windows were locked so we had to call a locksmith.

Surprisingly, he didn't even ask to see the police report. He took our payment and just opened the door. My sisters and I prayed before entering the home. We had no idea what to expect. There was a neighbor who met us outside and offered her condolences. She shared with us that my nephew, Shay's son, came to her house to call the police afterwards, but he only said my sister was sick. But she knew something was off. She shared other disturbing stories with us about previous incidents and we all just cried. Why didn't Shay tell us what was going on? Why wasn't she honest? We could have helped, if only she had let us!

Once we opened the door, we realized the power was off which was weird. I called the detective to ask why, and he said it was off when they got there. There was no way my sister was living in a house without power. She worked from home, and we saw her live on social media earlier that week. So, I called Georgia Power to find out who serviced the area. The electric company shared that the power had been turned off two days ago. It was a pre-payment plan and they shut the lights off for non-payment. So, I started to dramatically play out in my head how my sister's final hours were. I had to stop! I had to get myself together. We explained to the customer service person what happened and that we needed light to get everything moved out. The representative was very sympathetic and was willing

146

to assist me. I paid the bill to get it turned on for the next few days.

When the door opened, it was like a horror movie. I had to gather myself as I looked at blood on the floor and down the steps to the garage where he left her. The detective had explained that he was trying to get her in her car but could not lift her lifeless body. The car was still there and there was lighter fluid waiting in the back seat. I can't believe my nephew, the grandson of Jerome Alexander, had done this to his own mother.

My close friends and my sisters were with me. We all got the cries out that was needed, but we quickly pulled ourselves together as we went in her office to start packing up her belongings. We sang gospel songs and prayed the entire time. Momma and Kathy kept calling Trinnett and April to check on me, but I was clearly in a zone. After cleaning and packing downstairs, we knew we had to go upstairs where the murder took place, but we were all too distraught. Momma begged me not to go in Shay's room. We needed to leave and take a break, so we did.

We were told that there were companies you could call to clean up after a murder. So, we called several while we were out. We needed gloves, shoe coverings, and mask if we were going to go through the crime scene. I couldn't believe what we were out doing. We just parked and cried asking God to give us strength. It was an emotional rollercoaster. There was a service rep from a company that agreed to meet us at the house to inspect it for us and give us a price. After the inspection, he shared with us that the owner would have to sign off and it would cost over $5000! I couldn't believe it! He said that the floors needed to be pulled up and he said blood was all over the master bedroom walls and even in the bathroom. I told him I'd contact the homeowner and let him or her contact him directly. I just wanted my sisters' belongings and that was all that mattered.

I called my husband and cried. I told him I couldn't go in that room. He quickly said, "Give me a few minutes let me find someone." My sister-in-law agreed to come and clean out Shay's room, so we didn't have to. But we passed her room while cleaning out her workspace. April screamed out, "She loved us, she loved us," as she looked at our pictures lined up in the mirror of Shay's dresser. With all the problems I had with Shay over the years, and her ups and downs with the other sisters, our faces were the first faces she saw each morning and the last faces every night. I was so grateful to see those pictures. They gave me just a little comfort like hugging her the last time I saw her in person.

We went from room to room. We had gone there to pack her belongings, but first I had to try to put together what happened. That is what Daddy would have done. He would have wanted to know what happened to his child. He would have tried to save her like he did when he jumped in that pool to save me.

Each room in Shay's house told a story of her pain. When we got to her workspace, I had to pull myself together again. We all realized immediately that we were standing in possibly the beginning of the crime scene. Shay's hair was on the floor and just a small amount of blood. We then knew whatever happened between them must have started in that room and ended in the garage. After the shock of seeing everything in that room, I started going through her paperwork. Every piece of paper told another story. Shay was really struggling emotionally and financially. That crushed me all over again. I am telling you this not to harm my sister's spirit and your memory of her if you are family or a friend. I am telling you because I need to stop right here and help somebody. My sister was suffering in silence! I need to help someone else's sister today! If you need help, tell someone. Please! Forget what others will say or what you've portrayed. My sister needed me

149

in ways that I know I could have helped her. But her pride kept her from reaching out. Instead, her pain led her to build a deeper wedge between us so that we didn't know what was truly going on. Was this her way of protecting me? I'm not sure but I didn't need protection. She did!

My sister's only son was apparently suffering with mental illness. She was a smart woman, and she was writing and calling places all over Georgia trying to get help for him. The detective shared with me he had been in a mental health center and had only been home a day before the murder. We were not talking, so I knew none of this information. I had only seen him twice in 2016 - the day before her wedding and the wedding day. I knew something was a little strange, but I could not quite put my finger on the problem. She wouldn't share anything about him. We had just reconnected, so again, I didn't want to push. I learned later that he had been in and out of men's shelters since he was a teenager. Pretty much being homeless. But Shay seemed embarrassed to talk about it, so none of us brought it up unless she said something. She only told me that not having his father in his life really messed him up in high school. He was a star athlete, then unexpectedly, he no longer wanted to play sports and started acting out.

From the looks of all the paperwork, my sister recently had gotten her son to move to Atlanta with her. It was shortly before she stopped talking to the family again. Was this why she blocked us all? Was she trying to hide what was going on with him? Was she ashamed of his problems? Our last argument was about an unplanned Thanksgiving meal! It wasn't even a real plan. I happened to be in my hometown days before Thanksgiving and convinced my sisters to all make a dish. It was the silliest disagreement because I had only spent Thanksgiving with Shay twice in over 20 years. Surely there had to be more to her anger. I was planning to spend a week with her before Christmas. She never mentioned her son being there. Of course, because she was angry, I was uninvited. This bothers me tremendously to this day. I wish I had known. Maybe, just maybe, I could have helped her. Every emotion a person can have, I experienced while I was in her house.

After we left Atlanta, the pain of planning her funeral with her daughter began. My sisters helped so much, and that made me feel much better. Her favorite football team was Florida State University, so we all decided to wear garnet and gold. She was a die-hard fan! Some family tried to convince me to wait another week so that others could attend. Well, you know how I feel about a repast and the big show of it all. So, NO! I needed closure and so did her daughter. I planned the funeral for the following week. Luckily, I did because the next week, the world was on lockdown due to the pandemic! I could not have imagined not being able to say goodbye to my sister for months on end. I'm so thankful I went with my gut to get it done. So many wanted to share stories and memories about my sister. Classmates, her old boss, Ben Crump, and other legal professionals came to celebrate her life. They talked about what a wonderful employee and friend she was. Of course, many talked about her love for college football. That made me smile and cry at the same time. Football was a mutual passion of ours. My other sisters were uninterested so who would I be able to trash talk with? Shay had so much potential, and just like that, she was gone.

After her funeral, I just tried to pick up the pieces. I still do not know all the circumstances of her death, and I do not know if I will ever know or if I even want to know. The one thing I know for sure is I miss my sister. I miss the good times and I cry that we had so many troubled times.

I think about my sister's childhood and how everyone was always arguing and fighting because of her actions, which now I feel were cries for attention. She was a broken little girl who became a broken woman. Everyone was mad when Shay and I were kids, and guess who suffered? Shay suffered and I did.

The moment she threw the grits at me, she should have been put in counseling with all the adults. My sister was clearly having anger issues even as a child because everything set her off. Her parents, meaning my dad and her biological mother, were responsible for getting her the help she needed.

I need people to understand that Shay was a victim. She was a victim of her parents' divorce and broken relationship. She needed counseling early on. She and I needed counseling as adults. She was so angry about past pain and experiences that she missed the opportunity to love and be loved by her family. I am writing this to SAVE SOMEONE ELSE'S SISTER OR BROTHER. This chapter might save you! If you see a loved one in trouble, get them help no matter how much they resist. When you see a child acting out, seek professional help. Don't discount their behavior as just a "bad child" or even spoiled. There may be more to it than just what you see on the surface.

On March 6, 2020, when that phone rang, it was just too late. Shay was gone. My heart dropped. I kicked, screamed, and tried to make sense of losing my sister. I still scream and try to make sense of that night. I try to make sense of our life as sisters and where it all went wrong. I'm still going through so many stages of grief.

When my spirit was calm, I went into a rather quiet mood. Why didn't we stop fighting? Why did I let years go by and not reach out to her. When she died, we were not talking. If I had not run into her weeks prior, we would not have been speaking at all. There was something very wrong in my sister's life. She was crying out for help, and I could not hear her because of the arguments and stubbornness we both shared. I had the time and financial resources to provide counseling for us. I do not want others to feel this kind of pain. I have learned a valuable lesson from her life and death. I have learned to not be silent when you think someone you love is in trouble.

The past couple of years, I've really had time to think about my relationship with my sister. Sometimes anger takes a peep in because I know that some bystanders played a role in destroying our relationship. Of course, some people live for drama. They are miserable and want others miserable too. So, they saw a weakness in me and Shay's relationship, and they used that to manipulate her. What people don't know is after my wedding in 2000, Shay disappeared from my life without a trace. There was no argument or disagreement. I had no idea why she just changed her number and none of us could contact her. I thought she was dealing with the grief of losing our dad and their relationship. We knew she attended law school in Tallahassee, but we didn't know how to reach her. That was before social media. I received a call in 2004 from a creditor looking for her. I finally was able to find her using information that they shared with me, and we reconnected. I just wanted to spend time with her. After losing our dad, I felt we should have had each other to lean on and I missed my niece and nephew. I shared a little about my marriage and that I was considering divorce and wanted to see her. She kept making excuses to see me so again, I didn't push.

We would talk every few months and then she planned to meet my cousin, Alexis, and I in New Orleans for the Essence Festival in 2005. I had just moved there and offered to let them to stay with me. She agreed and was supposed to meet me and Alexis at a restaurant once she got in town. We kept trying to reach Shay that day and she never answered our calls. She would only text, so we knew something was up. We finally gave up and it was another 3.5 years before I heard from Shay again. This was our cycle. Every time we would build our relationship, she would pull away. These were troubling signs that I should have recognized were a cry for help.

I just want to encourage each one of you to be vigilant if you feel you have a family member that you feel might be depressed or may be having problems. Not just with your family, but with your friends and co-workers. If you think something is wrong, then something is wrong. We are... our sister's keepers.

CHAPTER 13

THE POWER OF PRAYER AND GIVING

I have a praying mother! I could really end this chapter with that one line. "I have a praying mother." From the time I was old enough to understand words, I understood that she was praying for me. I understood that she was praying for Kathy, and all the children who would eventually call her mother. She was also praying for my Daddy to turn his life around. Before I had ever heard of a "prayer closet" I watched my mother lay on the floor and cry out to God.

I can remember things happening in the family, and other people would be so upset. Not Momma! I could see it in her eyes that she was about to go tell God! She would immediately start to pray. If someone were sick, Momma would call out their name. She could stay in prayer mode for hours if that is what she deemed necessary. I witnessed her wake up praying and go to bed praying. To this day, she remains prayerful throughout the day. Now, with her having access to church services via YouTube or social media, she just puts in her earplugs and goes from one service to the next. My sisters and I always laugh about it. "Where's Momma? At church in her ear!"

When I was a little girl, I knew she was praying a lot, but I did not really understand why. Over the years, I have come to realize that it was only God and the prayers of Momma that kept me safe. Because of her prayers, my illness has never manifested to what others said it would be. It was the prayers of Momma that set the example for my father to join church and become the Christian man he became. The night Momma walked out that door and carried me to revival, may have felt like a divide between my parents, because Daddy refused to go. In essence, he was at home having his own revival. He stayed behind and prayed for me just like the people at my uncle's church were doing. He stayed behind and asked God to heal my sick body, and that is what God did.

The thing about Jerome Alexander was you could not tell him anything! You had to show him. He watched Momma live the life of a Christian woman all those years. He watched her go to church on Sunday and throughout the week. When he cried out to God, it was for me, because Daddy knew that prayer changed things. He knew because he had witnessed Momma's prayers for years. I came home healthy and stronger, but Daddy was healthier too. Although he was always short tempered and argumentative his approach changed after he gave his life to Christ.

I often think about how his Christian life brought him not only closer to God, but also to church. He was at church not just on Sunday, but all the time for every function. When I was younger, sometimes I was so frustrated about how often we attended church. But now that I'm older, I'm so thankful for that foundation. It helped mold me into the woman I am today. If he had not started coming to church more, I do not know if he would have ever gotten to know Trinnett, Trina, Delores, or April well enough to let them live with us. That is just how God worked out my parent's lives. He showed them the goodness of faith and prayer, and they passed that knowledge down for generations to come.

Because my parents showed me the power of prayer, that is what guides my life today. Yes, I fall short sometimes, but I always go back to God. I always go back to prayer. I start my day with prayer. While everyone else in my house is fast asleep, I am praying. Sometimes, if I am tired, I will go back to sleep, but I always wake up around 4:30 a.m. for my quiet time. That is my time to talk to God. People ask me what I pray for and about. Let me tell you! I pray about everything, and I pray for everyone. I do have special prayers for my family and people I know are going through things they might feel are out of their control. I do not feel anything is out of the control of God. It might be out of our hands, but not God's. Yes, there

159

are times that I've prayed for something, and it hadn't gone the way I wanted. But I'm a believer that regardless of how things currently look or feel, because of my relationship with God, I always know that he is working the situation out for my good.

This is the way I look at life, and I include this thought in my prayers. Every day is a chance for new mercies and new grace. Every day that I am alive, I have a chance to ask God for his help, his forgiveness, and his new guidance. When I feel I have done something wrong, I ask God for forgiveness instead of letting it linger inside of me. Not only do I ask God for forgiveness, but I go to the person or people I may have wronged and ask them for forgiveness. "I am sorry" are three very simple words. If I apologize to someone, it is for two reasons. First, I want the person to know I meant them no harm, and second, I also believe that asking people for forgiveness is a type of freedom for yourself. Sometimes you ask people for forgiveness, and they might say "No." Do not worry, just know that you did the right thing!

Now, that should work both ways. When people do things that I might feel are wrong and they apologize, as a Christian I must accept their apology. Forgiving someone does not mean you have to invite them to Sunday dinner. It means you have freed yourself from ill will towards them. You might be asking yourself how you get to this point. For me, it is the power of prayer. It is knowing that I can't ask God to forgive me when I fall short or mess up and not do the same for others. No, I'm not God, but I have him in my heart so I'm always reminding myself to be careful and not to be dismissive when others make mistakes.

The more I pray, the less I worry. I encourage you to do the same. There is a special place in your home that you can call your quiet place. Pray there! Listen quietly and hear his voice to lead and guide you. If you need to cry sometimes, it's okay.

I am a walking, living miracle, so I know that prayer truly works. I know the doctor told my parents I would never do anything normal teens and young adults did. They even told them that I might have a disability. I know Momma and Daddy said "no" to the doctors and "YES" to God. I know the power of prayer!

There have been dark situations in my life when only God could have saved me mentally and emotionally. I've never wanted to give up because the fight in me was to push through my pain to reach my final purpose. Sometimes, we go through things to help and minister to others. Because of our strength and faith, God can trust us to assist others who may be weaker in those given areas. Regardless of your religion or faith, I encourage you to meditate and believe that your situation will get better.

In addition to having a strong prayer life, I'm very passionate about serving and giving in the community. Throughout my Christian upbringing, I was taught to tithe and give offerings within the church. It was the foundation of sowing and reaping. When you give to others, you will be blessed because of your thoughtfulness and generosity. As I got older, I recognized that it was necessary to give outside of the church walls as well. Yes, the ministry I fellowship needs me to contribute so that they can do work in the community. People go to churches when they are in need. Whether it's money, shelter, food, or clothing. But I too can-do work outside of those walls.

My parents not only opened our home to my god sisters, but my parents were also foster parents at times. Soon after my father died, my mother began fostering consistently until she remarried. When she first became a foster parent, I thought it was because she was lonely. But she said her heart went out for the children who didn't have someone to love them daily. Momma had the room in our home and in her heart to extend love to them. My sister and I were one hundred percent supportive of her. Meeting and spending time with kids who had some horror stories and trauma at such a young age made me want to do something once I got older and had stability. The foster care system is broken. The funding and overall politics of it all makes me sick to my stomach. These children don't deserve the lack of attention that they must live with.

My husband and I contribute to several programs monthly, to ensure that children have activities throughout the month. Whether it's movies, bowling, skating, or something fun to just be a kid. My foundation is always looking for children and single mothers to support in many ways – through tutoring, coats during the winter, and of course Christmas. To think of a child waking up on Christmas with nothing breaks my heart. Being a blessing to children and families is no longer optional for me. It's a part of the fabric of who I am, that was passed down to me from Momma and Daddy. We often make contributions in total secrecy.

You might not have the means to open your home or financially support someone in need. But we all have time! Make a commitment to at least volunteer at soup kitchen or fold clothes at a clothing bank quarterly. Taking the time to serve others is such a fulfilling experience. When I'm feeling at my lowest, I think about others in need and how blessed I truly am despite the situation in front of me. It's a reality check.

CHAPTER 14

FINANCIAL BOUNCE BACK

During my childhood, my family was considered middle class. Of course, as a child I did not know what that meant. I just knew that our needs and wants were met as children. I never heard my parents say, "we can't afford that" or "no because it costs this." Now, they may have said, "no," but it was never in response to the price. Well at least that's what we thought. Now understand, we weren't rich, but they always made a way to give us our needs and most of our wants. I'm sure they had private conversations about the cost of items, so even if something was a knock off, we felt accomplished. We were kids. You can take a kid to the dollar store and say get whatever you want, and, in that moment, the kid feels rich! When I hear friends and family members telling their children they cannot have things they are asking for because they do not have money, it saddens me. Because I do not think a child should carry the weight of their parents' financial struggles. Those words, "we are broke," are very heavy for a child. They don't want to see their parents struggle nor do they want to feel like they are a part of the struggle.

I remember one of my younger relatives telling me she wanted a certain doll, but her mommy said it costs too much and she could not afford it. The look in her eyes was not about being able to get the doll, it was the burden of wanting her mother to have more money. That broke my fragile, little heart. She realized at three years old that her family was financially struggling. At that point, she was careful what she asked for because she did not want her mother to be sad. What a tremendous burden for a child.

I do not know how hard my father really had to work to become a successful black man in Corporate America. I do know that he was determined, just like Momma, to work hard and have nice things for our family. I watched my aunts and uncles also worked extremely hard to provide for their children. I saw that at an early age, so that is what I wanted for myself by the time I was in middle school. I wanted to be able to live where I wanted, drive what I wanted, and travel! By middle school, I was also 100 percent sure that I was going to college. At that time, a better education meant more opportunities. More opportunities meant better pay and living well. That is what I saw every day of my young life, and that is what I wanted for myself as an adult.

My parents made it clear that if I wanted their lifestyle, I would have to work for it. People call me spoiled, but I was spoiled from their love and affection. When it came to money, by the time I was a teenager, I worked for it. There were no allowances in our house. You lived there; you did chores there. Yes, we had chores, but we did not get paid for them. It was called responsibility. They made it clear; you sleep here, you clean here.

When I was in the ninth grade, I decided I was old enough to work in my Aunt Cynthia and Uncle Johnny's restaurant. I somehow convinced them that I would make the perfect hostess on the weekends. Their restaurant was so busy that they let me start working right away. Within one day, I was taking orders and serving customers as a waitress. Wait! This was not the original plan. I lasted about three months. I knew the service industry was not for me. My Aunt Cynthia is the ultimate hustler, and she was working me in every corner of that restaurant. That is when I learned to take care of my business. She worked just as hard as the staff, and she excepted the same from us. She also taught me that in business, there is no favoritism. Make sure if you hire a family member, you have the guts to fire a family member.

Okay, the restaurant business was not for me, but I was going to keep working. By the 11th grade I had enough credits to graduate, so I could leave school early and participate in the work program. Daddy was helping us find jobs, and he allowed me to work for Unisource, which was a paper wholesale manufacturer. I worked in a warehouse and would check in all the drivers and complete inspection audits. I was sixteen working with men around 30 years old or even older. The conversations I overheard were not for a 16-year-old, but I was nosey. I would put on headphones but play no music. They didn't want me listening to their conversations, and they were very respectful because they knew my Daddy was that man who would come into my job and take care of business, if you messed with his daughter. He sometimes came early and sat in the parking lot. I didn't understand it then but now I do. This is when I stop and say it again… he was a protector. I felt protected at home, school, and work. Every little girl should have that feeling. Every now and then, Daddy would just pop up on my job and give me and my friend a ride home. We had transportation with another friend who had a license, but Daddy wanted those men to know he existed.

When I started getting paid, I was so excited. Because Daddy worked for Southern Bell, Momma took me to the Florida Telco Credit Union to open my first checking and savings account. She had been in the banking industry before working for our church. She was the first African American banking officer for the financial organization that she worked for. She helped me to understand the importance of taking care of my finances. I've never seen someone count money like her! So, she was very skilled with teaching me the importance of balancing my checkbook and keeping my debits vs. credits logged with every transaction, even minor ones. There was no online banking then. Wow! I am realizing my age at this very moment. Imagine the world today with no online banking.

When I was seventeen years old, I changed jobs when Daddy asked one of his friends to hire me at the tax collectors, for the City of Jacksonville. That's when I learned the value of "who you know" matters. He had been personal friends of the tax collector for years and he got me and Kathy a job there.

It was noticeably clear to me by then that I was good with numbers, and I loved that job. I got along well with everyone there. Being the youngest in the office, I would often be called upon because I moved faster than a lot of the older ladies there. They all mentored me but did not treat me like a child. They celebrated with me every time I learned something new. I watched their every move, and I watched the way they cared about my growth. That is when I found out the value of recognizing your staff and team members.

I also learned another valuable lesson while working for the city. Yes, my dad had opened that door for me, but he could only open it! I had to keep it open and do well while inside. I did not want to just make him and Momma proud, I needed to do it for Earica! I took advantage of every opportunity that they made possible for me. I want all of you to strive to do the same.

The only thing I loved more than my job at the time, was payday on the 1st and the 15th! I still love payday! I work hard, and I love the reward showing up in my bank account. I loved watching my money grow. I was not a big spender. Instead, on payday I would have my parents drive me to the credit union and transfer my money from my checking account to my savings account. That was important for me. My dad never asked me about my balances, but Momma would. She still likes to ask!

The other thing that always happened on payday makes me sad when I think about it. I would bring my lunch, but I also went out to eat whenever I wanted to. Most of the time, I would ask the older employees if I could bring them something back. They only said yes on the 1st and the 15th. I brought my lunch sometimes, but they brought their lunch all the time. After a few pay cycles, I realized some could not afford to eat out other than those 2 days a month. Even then I was good with my money, so I was not wasting it in restaurants every day, but I did have the option to do so. However, if you work every day, you should be able to treat yourself when you want to. At least that's what I thought at age 17. So, when I asked if they wanted something and they said, "it's not payday," at a young age I didn't understand what that meant. Now, I understand that I was a teenager and living with my parents earning the same wages as men and women at least twice my age with families that was a harsh reality.

My parents talked to me about my money often. They wanted me to be responsible and they required me to buy my senior pictures. I purchased my clothing with my mom's approval of course. I trusted Momma's judgement. She was always one of the sharpest women I knew. She would be matching from head to toe. My dad required me to pay my tithes. It did not bother me because I believed in the concept. I still believe in giving. I saw how it worked for them and other family members. It became natural.

There has always been joy in working hard and having my own money. I have limits but helping or giving a gift to a friend or family member has never left me broke. If anything, it has helped me to build character as it relates to being a generous person. I have never missed that money any more than tithes at church. I could tithe, enjoy my young life, treat friends, and still save money. So, before I was out of high school, there were several financial concepts I learned, and those became basic skills to me. I learned the purpose of a checking account, savings account, tithing, and budgeting. In my guided journal, I share these concepts with you.

Now some of you may be reading this chapter and thinking, not everyone has these types of parental figure to help them. I understand that. And trust me when I say even some who do, still make poor decisions. Heck, even I did as you will soon see. But I think the valuable lesson I learned is it must be a choice. A decision to make better financial decisions. This starts in the mind by looking at your current environment, and deciding what you want in your future, whether your family had money or not. Some will choose to work extremely hard to ensure they have a better life than what their parents were able to provide for them.

Never accept your current circumstances as the be-all and end-all. You can make a change! With just a few minor financial adjustments, you could possibly change your life. A new career opportunity could be the chance you need. Meeting the right person with the right opportunity could set you up for unlimited success.

Once I got to college, I had a nice savings account established. I also applied for my first credit card on the campus of FAMU. It was a MCM telephone service account. Yes, I fell for the discounted services offer. I will tell you later what happened with this account. Shortly after, I applied for my first department store account at Burdines. You could not tell me anything! I never mentioned these cards to Momma or dad. I was having fun and enjoying the cards; something my parents did not tell me to do.

When I went home on the weekends, I noticed that something was off. Something, if not everything, was different. I made myself believe my parents were just cutting back, as retired people often did. Even when Momma traded her Lincoln Town Car for a Mazda Protégé, I thought everything was okay. Dad was no longer enjoying retirement but working as an investigator with the EEOC. He knew the commissioner in Tallahassee. Again, "who do you know" became important.

I did not ask enough questions and did not find out the truth until after Daddy died. Daddy received a lump sum of money when he retired. He was required to pay taxes on that money and failed to do so. This bill showed up and my parents had to make sacrifices that we (the children) were unaware of. Plus, with my dad's health failing, there were unplanned medical

172

bills that were piling up. I'm so thankful that they didn't share their financial problems with us. Can you imagine being that young, newly in college and having to worry about if your parents were going to be financially, okay? Let me tell you something, I had faith in my parents. So much faith, that I just could not imagine them not managing their money correctly. When they started selling fish dinners at church, I honestly thought it was because Daddy went fishing so much.

While in Tallahassee, my dad got me a job working as an assistant to a hearing impaired EEOC investigator. I learned so much about discrimination in the workplace. I would read the files to her, and she would transcribe them in braille. She was amazing! That is when I learned your disability does not have to define your level of success. Even though I worked part-time, I also started doing hair and making extra money. I did friends' hair while in high school but never charged them. But in college, I learned I could really make money because I had a natural gift when it came to hair.

As I told you in Chapter three, I asked my parents if I could stay at home and go to cosmetology school. Well, Momma previously owned a barber shop, so she recognized the potential earnings, but she wanted me to finish college. She said if I were able to handle both going to college and cosmetology school, I could stay home. It required a lot of hard work and time management to go to Florida Community College and cosmetology school while working full time at the tax collectors' office, but I did it.

What was harder than trying to do three things at one time, was not having my own car. Aunt Cynthia often let me drive her car, but that was getting old. One day, I was driving and saw a sign in front of the Hyundai dealership that said, "As low as $200." I pulled in and applied for my first car loan. I was nineteen, working full time, and had at least two years of work history and credit history. I left that dealership with a payment less than $300, Gap insurance, and $500 down. Oh hunny! I thought I was big stuff! I had a friend pick me up to take my aunt her car. We went back to get my new ride, and I rushed home to tell my parents.

I was so excited when I started telling them and trying to get them to walk outside to see my new Hyundai. Momma and Daddy were furious until they learned what my payments were. My dad calmed down and said I negotiated well after he saw the contract. My mom, however, was still on ten! She made it clear that I was not grown up yet and should have included them in this decision since I still lived in their house. Well, I wanted to beat my chest that day. I told her that was my car and not her responsibility, and I worked to make the payments. That was the wrong thing to say to Eara! Momma turned into a gangster. She made it clear that she would burst every window out that car, and as long as I had breath, I better not tell her about my money and what she couldn't do. My response was, "yes ma'am." I knew she was proud, but I was not going to push her any further.

After purchasing the car, my parents realized I really did understand business, and they wanted me to understand credit. But wait! You just got a good deal, so that meant you had credit that we did not know about! I had to come clean and tell them about the MCM and Burdines accounts. Momma did not break the windows out of my car, but she made me pay off both cards and she took my cards away. Everything was fine with the Burdines card, but five years later, the MCM card came back to haunt me.

Because I was being a fast teenager, the bill was not coming to my parents' house. It was still going to my old address at FAMU that I no longer had access to. Well, someone had somehow gotten a second card and was using it and stopped paying the bill. The monthly fees piled up, and I had no idea. Five years later when Joe and I tried to purchase our first home, that MCM card became an issue. I had a charged off balance that I knew nothing about. I was so upset. I had totally forgotten that the statements were being mailed to a PO box at the dorm. Whoever used it was clearly paying it fine when I purchased the car because it didn't come up. One day they just decided to stop, and that is when it came up on my credit report. Before that, I do not think I had ever even looked at my credit report. I thought that once Momma took the credit cards, everything was fine.

How can I fix this? After speaking with several people between MCM and the collection agency, they agreed on a settlement. I was able to pay a reasonable amount to have them remove this from my credit report. This cannot be real life. How often does this happen to people? Why is it allowed? Less than $800 of a debt I was not aware of and had not created myself, almost cost me my home. One of the most valuable lessons I learned during that season of my life, was to manage your bills and your credit. One mishap can ruin everything! I became laser focused on saving money and keeping my credit score high. Also, I pull my credit annually to make sure everything on there is accurate. Take that lesson from the book and use it as you will.

It was important for me to understand my credit score from that point on. After I started working in the banking industry,

I passed that knowledge on to every customer that would listen. I started taking every credit and lending course offered. I told them what every lender would look for. I told customers the questions they should ask and how the underwriter would make decisions based on that "story."

Being in the banking industry was an eye-opening experience. The color of your skin wasn't a part of the decision process, but the declines were higher amongst minorities due to the lack of education regarding the process. Unfortunately, minorities and underserved communities missed opportunities or were charged higher interest rates because of their poor credit. How can this be fair? People with more money and better living conditions get charged less. How can I change this? What can I do to educate these communities? If people understood their credit and how it works, we could change this cycle. The credit unions I worked for offered free workshops about first time home buying, and credit. Sadly, not many people of color showed up for these workshops. Why are those who need the information the most, not seeing the value of these free seminars? I felt that one day I would be able to help them.

Before I could teach others, I had to learn a valuable lesson of my own. I started telling you about what happened after Hurricane Katrina, but I wanted to save the details for this chapter. When I relocated to Atlanta, one of the things I wanted to do was get into real estate investing. I had seen it work for several family members, and I knew home ownership and real estate investment was key. After purchasing my townhome, I decided to purchase three additional rental properties in Metro Atlanta. What I had not factored in was the state of the economy at that time, and who was going to maintain the properties for me. It was a lot of work, and I had zero experience. Shortly after, the market crashed, my rental properties values plummeted. There was so much to be done and I drained my savings trying to do it all alone.

I started applying for credit cards and found myself over extended. Momma was doing everything she could to help me. I was only thirty-one and earning almost $90K annually. Why is this happening now? I was dating Brian, and things were going well. I cannot tell him that my credit is sinking, and I am drowning in debt. I cannot let my employer know what is happening. I am the one teaching the staff about credit. What will they think? Will they lose confidence in my abilities? From the outside, it looked as though I had it all together. Young, gifted, educated, and black! Powerhouse! I kept the appearance up for two years, and I finally made the decision to file for bankruptcy. I met a client who was a millionaire and he had filed bankruptcy twice. I felt comfortable with sharing my struggles with him, and he suggested I file for chapter 13. So, I quietly went to have a consultation with a firm. I still did not tell Brian out of fear he would reject me. I couldn't have been more wrong.

After getting the papers to move forward with the bankruptcy, I decided I better be honest with Brian. We had started talking about marriage, but he didn't know I was in financial trouble. One night I told him I needed to talk. I could tell he was a little nervous because of how I was acting. As I begin to tell him, the tears started uncontrollably rolling down my face. I was nervous that his perception of me would be forever tainted. His reaction was so different from what I expected. He grabbed me, held me, and said, "it's going to be okay. I wish you would have told me sooner. Maybe I could have helped you." I remembered earlier in our relationship him saying he did not want to be a landlord, so I never involved him. His patience and his kindness during that time made me love him even more! I thank God every day that I told Brian. I did not, and never want to, live my life in secret again just to look good to others.

After I talked everything over in detail with Brian, I filed bankruptcy and started to rebuild my financial life to what I knew it could be with a little work. About one month later, the organization that I worked for found out that I had filed Chapter 13 bankruptcy. Because I had a vehicle loan with them, even though I did not include them in the bankruptcy, because they were a creditor, they were notified.

Here comes Mr. "I want her hair like yours." He called my office phone and said he needed to see me. I went to his office, and he said the information was brought to his attention. He asked why I did not tell him. I responded, "Honestly, I did not feel it was any of your business. I was ashamed and it does not impact my job performance." He disagreed and felt that as an officer of the credit union, my financial status was important. He shared that our CEO would be made aware, and he would follow up. I was scared! I had given this organization my all for the last 5 years. Why would this be an issue? My job performance ratings were always above average or excellent. In addition to that, I felt like it was a personal attack. Our relationship was different after the hair incident. I was no longer his AACE!

That same week, the CEO and Human Resources VP, my boss, called for a meeting with me. The CEO was so arrogant. I had seen him act that way towards others, but this was my first personal experience. But for some reason I was unbothered. In fact, I was wanting him to terminate me. Clearly this organization did not see the value I added. He had the nerve to bring up that I had traveled to New York with my family for my niece's graduation, instead of paying on my debts. Who did he think he was talking to? All of Jerome Alexander's blood came rushing - through my veins. Not this time buddy! My boss knew they were pushing me too far, so she stepped in and tried to cool the temperature in the room! Honey, too late! I was Jerome hot! After the meeting, I knew my time was going to be limited there. I started secretly packing up stuff and emailing notes and documents to myself that I felt I would need later. My inner circle there knew what was going on. I had become good friends with some of the women there, and they thought I was overreacting. They could not imagine that company letting me go because they all knew how hard I worked.

All of this was going on during the time of my engagement to Brian, so I was not afraid of losing my job for two reasons. I had a plan, and a man who had my back. We were married in a small chapel in Orlando. The wedding chapel concept was so interesting and simple. So here I am on my wedding day, as happy as any woman could be, thinking about how I was going to start a wedding chapel business.

After our honeymoon, I told Brian about my idea and that I wanted to leave my job. After all we had gone through to get my finances back in order, he looked at me and spoke. "Go For It!" That is who I am married to. Thank you, God!

I did some research and realized the concept was a goldmine in Atlanta. I discussed the idea with two friends, Alysia, and Kimberly, who agreed to move forward with me. We did it! We opened a small wedding chapel in Duluth, GA. Luckily, this plan was in action because before I could quit my job, and with only three months of marriage, the company decided to let me go. In their meeting with me they stated I had "outgrown the organization." I was laughing in my head because I was thinking. You are correct… you are too small for me. I was out! They did me a favor!

I learned several valuable lessons in that process. No matter what you do for an organization, never think you are indispensable. Trust your gut and get your ducks in a row. You can do 10,000 remarkable things, but man will find one error, and judge your entire life based on that. If you die tomorrow, your job will be posted online before your obituary is. Remember that!

Being released from that job released me from so many weights around my legs. I notified my bankruptcy attorney of the termination; he resubmitted my file as a chapter 7 vs. thirteen. Once discharged, I was now completely relieved from those houses and the credit card. Thank God! What was meant to harm me, blessed me! Now it was time to rebuild.

The chapel business was going well, and we were making a profit within a few months. Not to mention the bank had to make a settlement with me after my termination. Brian and I did well without me working. A few months later, I was contacted by another institution, a competitor to the last, to come and start a lending training program for them. I immediately thought about how judgmental the last CEO was, and I did not want to ever feel like that again. I needed to be honest, and I needed to see if this would be a roadblock in my career. The COO was unbelievably kind and respectful. She thanked me for my honesty and said she knew what I could do. "I have seen your work and I understand life happens. This will make you an even better trainer in the industry." WOW! What a different response. She showed empathy as a leader. She listened. I knew I could learn a lot from her, and she was willing to coach me. So, I took the offer.

My friends and I decided to close the chapel. Alysia was pregnant with her second child, and I started a new job. We said we would do it again later, but God had another plan for all of us....

After a year of building a lending certification program at the organization, they were impressed with the results. I was offered the opportunity to manage their Home Equity department. I had no experience in this arena, but the COO trusted my abilities. She made me feel like superwoman, and I was not going to let her down! I was not going to let ME down. In my past as a loan officer, I had originated home equity loans and did some underwriting, so I was confident I would get the job done. The previous organization saw its highest lending growth because of my Home Equity closings so I knew the process.

As I was transitioning into the new role, the first mortgage manager abruptly left. The VP and the COO offered me the role to take on both departments. The salary was not something I could decline. I knew my life was about to change. Our lives as a new married couple were about to change. Brian was supportive and although I was a new stepmom, we agreed to make it work. My savings account was growing! My student loan debts were being paid down and my credit score was rising! I mean *really* rising!

A year later, I was promoted to Director which opened the door to bonuses I had never even imagined before. Oh' my God! Thank you for protecting me and thank you for the last organization letting me go. I would have still been there undervalued and underpaid for the work contributions I was making. Sometimes, God must force you out of situations. There is a plan and a process that we must trust. Shortly after my promotion, I was approved for a $400K + home, two years after filing for bankruptcy. There goes that faith and that power of prayer being activated once again. This taught me that you can always bounce back. Trials are not designed to break you but to make you stronger. Trust that when one door closes, another one opens. Your setback is your comeback. Have faith in God! Have faith in you! It is not over until it is over!

CHAPTER 15

BABY COLE

It is my belief that Brian and I have made good decisions as husband and wife and as parents. I am thankful that he is not a part-time husband who checks in and out emotionally. He is not only there for me but there for my Momma and my sisters too. God has blessed us in really getting to know each other and know what we need as a couple. I am thankful every day that we have secured our future financially and provide a stable environment for the people we love. Those are areas we have worked extremely hard on, and we can see our results clearly.

With all our blessings and good fortune, there are some situations we really can't control. The hardest thing I have ever had to fight for in my life is trying to have a biological child. I use the term biological because Bricen is my son in all the ways that matter, however, my love for him does not mean I do not want to give birth to a son or daughter of my own, with my husband.

There was so much love in our home when I was a little girl. I wanted to be a good mother, like my Momma one day. I wanted my children to have a good man as a father, just like my Daddy! I never discussed being a mother with my momma as a teen, or even as an adult, until I married Brian. It is strange when I think back on my relationship with my Momma. Strange because we talked about everything except the birds and bees. In my household it was just, "you better not do it." Unfortunately, sex education is not a priority in a lot of Christian households. We are just taught that the feelings and actions should be saved for marriage. Not that I disagree with those teachings, I just feel there must be more explanations. Children need to understand the consequences and how to protect themselves if they choose not to wait. They also need to understand that the physical feelings they start to experience are natural.

When I started liking boys and became curious about sex, I talked to my sisters and best friend. Momma never said a word. It was left as "do not ask, do not tell." At that age, I knew I was not ready to have sex, but I was curious. I had questions. As years passed, I learned what I needed to know about sex and getting pregnant. At least what I thought I needed to know. Some of my friends had babies at an early age but I was not ready to be a mother. I had goals I wanted to accomplish. The plan I had for myself was to finish school, get married, and buy a house before becoming a mother.

This is another place in the book where you should pause. After I got married, I was on birth control but never asked my doctor if I could have children. Again... pause! I Should I have questioned my doctor about my body and becoming a mother one day. Some people conceive even while taking birth control. I still never questioned the fact that I didn't. I honestly thought it was God protecting me because He knew what the outcome was going to be with my ex-husband. At the ages of 22-25, not conceiving was not a big deal to me. Yes, I had sickle cell, but I knew that women with sickle cell gave birth, and the percentage that struggled were extremely low. I just continued with my annual visits to my OBGYN and received healthy results every year. I seemed perfectly fine to both me and my doctor.

After marrying Brian, we wanted a baby right away, and I stopped taking birth control. At that time, I had been on and off the pills for the last 15 years. I was told by friends, but not by my doctor, that sometimes it could take months for you to get pregnant if you had been on any type of birth control for prolonged periods of time. After a year of trying to conceive, I still was not pregnant, but I was not alarmed. I figured it was stress. As I mentioned in a previous chapter, I was terminated from my job shortly after we got married, and then I opened a wedding chapel business with a few friends.

A few months passed, and I started thinking about how I might need to slow down a little. At that point, I started to think about my health more. Maybe I needed to do some yoga or exercising. I was never really into fitness, but I would read that it helped others relax. So, another year passed and still no baby Cole. Okay Earica. You must be more intentional. I did not want to focus on timing when my husband and I made love, but my doctor told me that it would help. I started monitoring my ovulation. I had a calendar. I had an app on my cellphone. You name it, we were doing it!

I was trying not to let the situation bother me and I remained hopeful, but I had started to worry. By this time, my closest friends were having babies, and it looked like I was attending a baby shower every few months. Of course, everyone was asking, "when are you going to sit down and have some babies?" I would laugh, smile, and just say, "we are working on it." By this time, a few close friends had asked me to be their children's godmother. Of course, I said yes, but there was still no one calling me the one word I wanted to hear, which was Mommy!

After about twenty-four months, I had one question and one question only! What is wrong? That was my question to myself and my doctor. In 2014, I went to my gynecologist and told her that I was concerned and wanted to know why I was not pregnant. She recommended we do some preliminary testing to see if there were any obvious health deterrents. All my initial tests came back with positive results. I had two small cysts, but there was no concern to have them removed. She told me I was considered obese, but all these thighs and hips came from genetics, so I wasn't worried. My doctor did not see a problem. Of course, we assumed Brian was okay because he had Bricen. That one visit was the beginning of an eight-year journey of medicines, planning and unfortunately, failed pregnancies.

Within a few days, my doctor started me on Clomid which is used to treat infertility in women. It is supposed to stimulate and increase the number of hormones that support the growth and release of a mature egg, which is ovulation. After four months of taking Clomid, monitoring my ovulation, and putting my husband on a time machine, I felt burned out physically and emotionally. Every month I prayed my period would not come. Every month it came, and I slipped back into sadness and asking myself why I could not conceive.

I finally decided to take a mental and physical break, and I did. The timing was off, and I just needed to relax. God will give me the desire of my heart is what I told myself. The break was good for me physically, but not mentally. My career was taking off, we had built a home together and life was going well. But wait…I am thirty-six and entering the danger zone for giving birth. There is nothing worse than that feeling of racing against time. Racing against the clock to be a mother.

Before my 37th birthday, I decided to go back to my gynecologist to see what we could do next. She recommended I see an infertility specialist. My heart dropped! I knew what that meant. She had done all that she could do to help me. I needed a specialist. Does this mean I may not have children? Why is this happening to me? Why are family and friends all around me conceiving, but I cannot? Is God punishing me for something I did in my past? How could this be happening? Will I not be able to give Brian another child? Will I not have someone to leave my legacy to? Will my Momma not have the opportunity to play with my babies? When I tell you that all those questions were flashing through my head, I mean all of them. I was heartbroken.

Just before going to see the specialist, my husband and I decided to fast and pray as a family. We trusted God, and we knew He would honor our request. We started to prepare spiritually, mentally, and physically. During my initial consultation, there were so many tests and personal questions asked and answered. Brian could tell that I was overwhelmed.

After we left the specialist, we went to one of my favorite restaurants, PF Chang's, to regroup. We started talking about baby names and sharing good personal childhood stories. He was so positive, and although I was trying stay positive, I was terrified!

A few days passed and the results from the specialist arrived. I had polycystic ovary syndrome (PCOS). What is that and why am I just learning this information about my body? I have always gone to my doctors regularly. PCOS is a hormonal disorder common among women of reproductive age. Women with PCOS may have infrequent or prolonged periods, or excess male hormone levels. The ovaries may develop numerous small collections of fluid and fail to regularly release eggs. My insulin levels were high, but I did not have high blood sugar levels. I knew that my cycles had become heavier, but I assumed it was due to all the medicines I had been taking, and of course aging.

Once the specialist explained to us what was happening to my body, we had one question. So how do we treat this situation? How do we make me whole again so that I can be a mother? My doctor prescribed Metformin and I was required to take it three times a day. There was no recommended stop date at that time. She also recommended that we try artificial insemination in three months after starting the Metformin. We learned that our insurance did not handle the cost of infertility treatments, so we told her we would consider it and get back with her.

Meanwhile, while starting the treatment for my PCOS, Brian and I continued to try to conceive naturally. When I think about the things we did and the "tips" my friends would share with me, I blush. Let's just say we had a lot of fun, and I can't write it in this book because my Momma will know! Constant love making but still no Baby Cole! Ninety days passed, but no baby! At that point we decided to move forward with the insemination.

I had four artificial inseminations in 2016 with no pregnancy. I was devastated and internally fighting this battle that I shared with no one. I have no idea why I was embarrassed that I couldn't get pregnant. I have always believed I could do anything! Suddenly, I felt like a failure for the first time in my life. I could not do something that was supposed to be so natural. Ladies don't ever feel that way. It's not your fault. I promise you, it's not your fault. Don't carry the guilt and pain that I carried, when there is nothing, you could have done.

After I finished questioning my womanhood, I started doubting my marriage and being a stepparent. Is my husband having regrets about choosing me as a wife? Am I being the parent to Bricen I should be? Am I built to be a mother? There were so many emotions that were so difficult to share with others; emotions that I should have sought counseling for in addition to seeking couples counseling with Brian. Instead, I held it all in unless I was with my sisters or my girlfriends. Thank God for my beautiful circle of friends. They would allow me to just drown my sorrows with them. We would cry, laugh, and drink wine together!

Months passed and we finally started talking about In Vitro Fertilization (IVF). We had never discussed IVF because not having a "natural pregnancy" never entered our minds. I do not want to discourage anyone, but I do want to be honest. IVF is a very complex series of procedures. Because of some of the life choices we made, we were okay financially, but the mental and physical cost was high. We also had no idea how expensive this journey would turn out to be. The IVF procedure is designed to help orchestrate the fertility and pregnancy process. It's a combination of medications and surgical procedures to help fertilize an egg and implant it in the woman's uterus.

As we began doing research, we realized this was a costly process and it was not guaranteed. My age played a huge factor in my ability to even do this. The more I read about it, the more I wasn't sure it was something I wanted to do. Honestly, I questioned if I wanted to have medical expenses that could be well over $30,000 out of pocket!

After my financial struggles from the real state issues, I was financially back on my feet. I was working with a new bank, and I loved my job and my salary. I just could not be in debt again. In my business, I had seen mortgage home equity loans for people who were wanting IVF treatments. There is no way I was willing to go back in debt for a *maybe*. I needed time and space to really consider this program. Months past and when Brian would bring it up, my response would be, "I'm scared." "It's too much money." "Maybe it's not meant to be."

In 2017, I started a home-based business while still working full-time. We had extra money that we had no plans for, so we were able to pay cash for the procedures with no financial burdens. While making the decision to move forward with the IVF, I decided to take a job with another company. Suddenly, we were moving to Tuscaloosa, Al. That also meant we had to change all my doctors. January of 2018, we had our first visit at the infertility center in Birmingham. They were able to get all my medical records from the previous center to do an evaluation to confirm that I was a viable candidate for IVF treatment and evaluate if they would consider me as a patient. All my exams were great. The doctor did not see any reason I could not go through the program. I had to have a minor surgery in March, and they needed to wait until my body healed. I was on so many pills, and I started taking shots in my butt that left major bruises.

In addition to my sore body from the needles, my emotions were all over the place. That is when I started researching natural herbs to offset the mood swings. My poor husband learned how to best communicate with me during my mood changes. In October, my eggs had been fertilized with Brian's sperm and we were all set for the embryo transfer. My transfer was one of the most difficult experiences. I have a tilted uterus, so the position of the implantation process can be very taxing to my own body.

I was a little taken aback because every transfer story I had read or heard, included women who said it was quick and easy. Of course, not me! I cried like a baby and almost told them to stop. After about 30 minutes of them using various instruments to facilitate the transfer, they finally got it done. Brian was with me the entire time, and he could see my pain. He was doing everything to console me, and afterwards he just kept gently rubbing my hands. I was a total wreck when the procedure was over. After I pulled myself together, we went for lunch and then I went home to rest. I had mild cramping for the next 24 hours or so, but after that, I felt fine. Now here comes the hard part…. waiting to hear if the transfer was a success or a failure.

I was scheduled to return to the office for them to do a blood test regarding my pregnancy, almost two weeks after the transfer. You are encouraged not to take home pregnancy tests, so I followed instructions. When I went back to the doctor, they told us that the transfer was not successful. I tried to be optimistic, but I was so disappointed. I really felt like the doctor did not understand my body. Why was it such a difficult procedure?

Other positive things were going on in our lives and we had to make some decisions. In early 2018, I decided to leave Corporate America and become a full-time entrepreneur. We chose to move to Tampa, to be closer to my momma and Brian really loved Florida. I really wanted to try another IVF round at the same facility before having to start all over again.

Although we could not get the transfer done prior to moving, we flew back to Birmingham for a second try. This transfer was just as painful as the first. We stayed the night in Birmingham overnight so I could get some rest. Again, we waited almost two weeks before being tested at a local gynecologist that I had found in the Tampa area. I was driving to see one of my friends, and I pulled over into a grocery store parking lot when the phone rang. I will never forget her call, "Hi Earica, did I catch you at a bad time? I am sorry to inform you that there is no pregnancy." I let out a deep breath. She knew our plans were to find a local infertility center if this one was not successful. She wished us well and said if the new doctor needed to speak with her, just let her know. I hung up the phone as tears rolled down my face. I called my husband and heard his disappointment, but he said, "It is okay. Let's move forward with our plans." He was not ready to give up. I pulled myself together, but I was not ready to tell my Momma or sisters. I just talked to Brian, and we found comfort in each other. I also needed time to wrap my head around it all, it was a lot to process.

We found an infertility center in Tampa and tried to remain positive. Ironically, they had recently merged with the treatment center where we originally started the infertility journey in Atlanta. They also told us about a shared risk program which we had never heard of. So, when we scheduled our consultation, we wanted to make sure we learned more about the program. The doctor was nice. He showed empathy and listened to everything we had gone through over the last several years. He stated he needed to order all my files from the previous clinics and wanted to run some tests due to my age and my sickle cell anemia. He also felt like tests needed to be done on Brian since they were never done. He explained the shared risk program which gave us the ability to pay a lump sum of money upfront. If I qualified for the program based on all my health factors, they guaranteed a healthy pregnancy or my money back. Although the program was expensive, all I heard was *a promised* pregnancy. Brian and I left feeling optimistic and ready to get this baby on board.

So here we are now doing all the meds and shots for a third time. I use the word "we" because it was my body but our chance to have a baby. Brian was there every step of the way. While my body was going through another whirlwind, we were building a house, and then the Coronavirus world pandemic hit. The pandemic was a nightmare as thousands of people were dying weekly, it broke my heart.

Because of the pandemic, my procedure was postponed, and that was for the best. The medical world was adapting to all the changes and how to perform procedures safely. I would have to go to doctor appointments by myself. Brian would wait in the parking garage while I was having treatments or tests. It was recommended that I have another hysteroscopy exam for them to do a thorough check of my uterus and see if scar tissue was there due to the difficult previous transfers. But by this time, it felt good. It felt like the stars were aligned. We were in the final stages of building our home, and the timing just seemed perfect.

The transfer was scheduled for February 2021. This third transfer was not as difficult as the first two. But it was still painful. I was alone this time, but the doctors and nurses were supportive. After the transfer, I cried a few tears, but I was happy. This one really felt like "third time's a charm." I went home, and although I was told to take it easy, there was so much to do because we were weeks away from closing on our new home and moving in. We had to be out of the rental house in less than a month so, my momma and sister Kathy, came to the rescue. They helped us pack, and I would give directions. Although I would try not to move boxes, unknowingly, I found myself moving items I shouldn't have moved. But I felt different this time. I started eating different. Having weird cravings. My momma and sister would say, "oh yeah, you're definitely pregnant."

After about nine days and with a doctor's appointment two days away, I decided to stop by a pharmacy and get a pregnancy test. I did not tell Brian or anyone because I did not want them to discourage me from doing it. When I got home, I rushed to take the test and OMG! It was positive! I screamed and called Brian to show him the results straight away. I was so excited. He hugged me and we cried together. *FINALLY! WE ARE PREGNANT!!*

I called my mom, and she was so happy! My sisters were all ecstatic. After the doctor confirmed our pregnancy with a blood test, I sent all my best friends flower bouquets with a "Can't wait to meet you Tee Tee, from Baby Cole" note. They were all so excited! We decided to keep it just among our inner circle for the first trimester, but let me tell you, I started walking pregnant. Picture me with a belly that existed prior to being pregnant and rubbing my belly and back as if I were 7 months along. I started ordering baby stuff and writing in my journal. I went to baby stores looking at cribs. Finally, it was happening for us! We were going to be in our beautiful home in a few weeks, and I could start decorating the nursery. This was the most exciting time in my life. I was already planning how we would announce it. Where was the shower going to be? Baby names, etc.

The doctor scheduled me to return in 5 weeks for my first checkup and ultrasound. I had to continue all my meds and shots, but I did not care. Whatever it took, I was going to do it.

Our home closing got pushed back several times. We told the builder we had to be out by March 31st. That was the day of closing, but it was also the day of our 5 weeks checkup. No worries, we would make it work. We had movers prepared to start packing stuff, and I had a meeting out of town the weekend before closing in Orlando. The beds were already taken apart for the move, so I stayed at my momma's house that last week.

I was happy about my baby, my family, and our new house. I was trying not to do too much but decided to drive to Hobby Lobby to find a picture. As I got out of my SUV, I felt wet. There was something running down my leg. It was blood! I tried not to panic because I had read that sometimes there's light bleeding early in the pregnancy. I went back to the car and called Brian. He was calm and told me to call the doctor's office, so I did. The nurse asked me was I in pain, and I said "no," but I felt like I was sitting in a pool of blood. She told me to go to the nearest Emergency Room and once I am checked in, to call her.

"This cannot be happening." Was all I kept saying as I drove to the emergency room. I called Momma, and she was not nearby. She told me she would call my cousin, which is also her Pastor, to meet me there. We did not know if anyone would be able to come into the hospital because of COVID. I made it to the emergency room and by this time, I knew something was seriously wrong. There was still no pain, but I felt like blood was everywhere. I could not find a parking space, so I decided to just pull up behind an ambulance. I got out the car and walked through the door and blood went all over the floor and in my shoes. I started screaming and nurses were coming from everywhere. I kept saying, "I'm pregnant, save my baby please!" It was like a horror movie. They got me in a wheelchair, and the panic in the other people's eyes around me was something I will never forget. Everyone knew it was not good. I told them I had an IVF transfer and how many weeks I was in my pregnancy. They got me out of all the bloody clothing and wanted to make sure I was comfortable. I didn't care about comfort. I was fighting for the life of my baby. One of the nurses was cleaning me up and put a large blood clot in a cup. I looked down at the cup and then I looked at her. I asked was it my baby and she said they did not know, but she would take me for testing. I was devastated!

My cousin called and prayed with me and told me he was on his way. He knew by him being a minister, they would let him in even if they would not let Brian in. They both arrived around the same time, and they both were allowed inside. We were all nervous but trying to remain positive. The nurses came to take me for an ultrasound. They kept asking was I in any pain. The answer was still "no." After the ultrasound, we went back to the room and waited. About an hour later, the doctor came in and asked when I passed the clot, before or after the ultrasound. I said before, and he wanted me to make sure. "Sir, I remember every moment over the last couple hours." He said that the fetus was still there but that he could not guarantee that I would not miscarry. But as of now, I had not. He urged that I rest the next few days and stick with my appointment in 5 days for another ultrasound. We all were so relieved. That was terrifying! What was that? I needed to understand. He spoke with my nurse from the IVF clinic, and they were talking about subchorionic hemorrhage. I had never heard of this, but I was about to spend my days and nights researching it.

My IVF clinic nurse explained that sometimes subchorionic hematoma is high in IVF pregnancies and frozen-thawed embryo transfers. I really did not understand, but she said it happens sometimes, and I may bleed a few weeks or a few months, but some women who have experienced it still have healthy babies. I told myself to remain positive. Everyone else told me to remain positive, but there was a feeling of uncertainty that I could not shake.

I had a business event scheduled in two days that I could not cancel. Momma and Brian asked me to reschedule it, but there was no way. People were flying from across the country. I would make it work, and Kathy was going to be with me to ensure I always rested and stayed seated. Just as the nurse stated, I continued to bleed, but it was more like a monthly cycle. My IVF doctor called to check in a couple times and said these things happen sometimes but let us be optimistic. I was starting to feel better because in most of the articles that I read with miscarriages related to subchorionic hemorrhage, there was pain, and I still had no pain.

It was hard, but I moved forward with the event for the weekend, and Kathy never left my side. When we were finished, she came home with me to help finish the move, and they wanted me to stay in bed! I stayed at my mom's while Brian worked with movers to get everything out of the old house and into the garages of the new home. The builder allowed us to start putting items in there since we were closing in two days.

My closing date and my ultrasound were the same day. Of course, the clinic still had rules that Brian could not come in with me, due to the pandemic. So here I am laying back for my first ultrasound, and my husband could not be with me. I was ready to video it for him once we saw the fetus. After the nurse moved around my uterus several times and was not saying much, I knew something was not right. She then pulled back and said, "I'm sorry Mrs. Cole, there is no viable fetus." I balled uncontrollably. She told me to call Brian in. He came up and we held each other. My baby was gone. There is no pain like what I felt at that moment. Why? What did I do? This could not be happening. The doctor wanted to see us both. He showed complete empathy and told us he understood but it was too soon to worry. This was my first pregnancy, so now we know I can get pregnant. We are going to get this baby here. I was overwhelmed with grief, but I pulled myself together to walk out the office. How do I tell my Momma? This is month end, and one of the busiest days for me. We close in less than 3 hours on our home.

I called Momma and Kathy to let them know. They were both devastated. I could not tell anyone else right now. I had cried all I could cry, and honestly, there was so much to do. I had to regroup. We went to the bank to get the wire transfer completed for closing. We went to the closing and shook everyone's hands and smiled and had small talk. My realtor brought up how exciting it was to get a new home and a baby. I smiled and said it was great. Closing was delayed another two hours, so we were stuck in this office with these people, and I just wanted to curl up in bed and sob. My phone was also buzzing like crazy with business texts and notifications.

We finally finished the closing, and we pull up to our incredible new home. Wow! What a blessing. My emotions were all over the place. How does God bless us with this but take our baby the same day? No Earica! It's wrong to think like that! You are blessed! You will get pregnant again. Enjoy this moment. I went in the house and started unpacking. Momma came over and asked if I was I okay. I told her and Kathy I did not want to talk about it. Let's just unpack instead.

I spent the next couple of weeks unpacking, organizing, and decorating like a wild woman. I sent a text message to my inner circle with a simple message, "I lost the baby, I am okay but not ready to talk about it. I love you." I got the quick response back with "I love you" and "let me know if you need me," etc. I did not respond. I threw myself into my work and my home like a mad woman. My god-sister April would send me texts and I would not respond. Finally, I agreed to let her see "the house" if she promised no baby talk. I knew she and Brian were in cahoots together, but she is my emotional sidekick. If I do not let her in during those dark times, she carries the load with me. I needed her to see that I was in a good place.

Life went on. I did not talk about my miscarriage for months. When I finally decided to talk about it, I decided to use my platform on social media to put it out there. Maybe, just maybe it would help someone else if I told a little of my infertility journey, but not too much. Man, I was overwhelmed with messages from followers, friends, and complete strangers. So many women shared that their story and how powerful my message was. This was so unexpected. I gave infertility and IVF a face to some who had never heard of these stories. Is this why I miscarried? Did God need me to help others who may not be as strong as me or who may not be able to afford programs like this? How can I help? How can I bring awareness to this? What is next? My husband was torn about me sharing our story, but he saw that it was something I needed to help heal. So, he gave me his blessings, and we started sharing more on my family's YouTube channel, *Eara's Girls*. Now that people know what I am trying to accomplish, I decided to take them with me on some parts of the journey that I felt comfortable to share.

When it was time for my next IVF in the summer of 2021, I had to prepare myself. There was more going on in my life than my desire to become pregnant. I had been experiencing social media attacks by complete strangers. This drama was causing a lot of sleepless nights, anxiety, and headaches. I was not feeling like myself. I needed to use all my positive energy on me and baby Cole.

No matter what was happening, I just kept going. We started the shots and medications again. It was now time for transfer number 4. Whew! I never imagined these many rounds. I really had no idea. This transfer was not a pleasant experience at all. It felt like the transfer in Alabama. It was very painful! I decided to rest more this time. Well, I was forced to rest by my family and friends. Those two weeks did not feel like the last pregnancy. I started taking pregnancy tests after day five. All the tests were negative, I decided to go ahead and tell Brian that I had taken a test and it was negative. His response remained the same. It's okay! We've got this!

Brian was trying to help me, but his response was not helping or comforting me. His body was not going through this taxing process. He was not worried about never being a parent or having an heir because Bricen was his biological child. I was very detached from him this time. When it was time to go to the doctor for my blood test, I told him I could drive myself. He had no clue that I was bothered or what I was thinking. After the blood test, I came home and went to work. I knew the results. I did not even answer the phone when the nurse called. I sent her to voicemail. Once I decided to check the voicemail, it was the results I expected. Am I done? Do I want to this again? NO was my first thought.

My doctor set up a conference call with me and Brian to discuss the next steps. During that call, I just listened intently to every word. We all agreed when to try another round, but I was exhausted by it all. I started a weight loss program and wanted to lose about ten pounds. It was that time again. Transfer five. I honestly just wanted to get it over with. I went back through the same regiment. This transfer was a little smoother but still there was difficulties.

About three days after this transfer, I started eating everything! I was craving collard greens with hot peppers every day and Momma was happy to oblige. I was tired a lot. My lower back was on fire. I ordered a special pillow that I preferred at night. It would wrap it around my entire body because it was like a cloud. Oh boy, Earica! You are pregnant. I purchased a few homes pregnancy tests, and they all came back positive every day. I was so excited! Brian was so happy! This is it! We were having a baby!! I gained those ten pounds back in two weeks, and I was happy to be gaining weight. I was so excited when it was time for my test because I knew the answer was yes! We just need confirmation. Later that day, we got the exciting news that we were pregnant again!

I did not tell as many people this time, and I still wanted to wait until after the first trimester to make an announcement. But I was wobbling around, eating, and growing a belly. I started taking weekly pictures to journal it all. Every time I went to the bathroom, I kept checking for blood. I was so nervous, but there was no blood. This was really happening. I was preparing for the holidays and could not wait to share the news with my inner circle.

It was time for our 5-week ultrasound. Because of the doctor's schedule, we went at 6 weeks. Brian was allowed to come in this time. We were nervous but hopeful. The technician started the test. This time she was circling and marking things. She showed us the gestational sac, but she could not see an embryo. She told us not to panic and that sometimes it takes a few more weeks. When we left, of course I googled everything and was so anxious. They rescheduled us to return in 10 days. Over the next several days, I felt my body changing. I was no longer having the cravings or pain in my back that I did the first several weeks. This was not a good sign for me. I tried to remain hopeful, but I was also beginning to realize that this may be another miscarriage. I did not talk about it much and I just kept going on day-to-day as if everything were okay. When it was time for that visit, Brian and I woke up and got dressed, but you could tell we were both feeling pessimistic.

Once we arrived and went back to the room, we took deep breaths, and she began with the ultrasound. After a couple minutes, she said, "I'm sorry, there is no growing embryo." I honestly do not remember crying. She said she was going to get the doctor. Brian held my hand and kissed it. I did not say anything. I was just ready to go home. When the doctor came in, I said, "This isn't working for us, is it?" He was his normal hopeful, yet empathetic, self. When he started telling us our options to terminate the pregnancy or allow me to naturally dispose of the baby, I was quiet. He said it may be painful, but it was my decision. We decided to schedule a D&C to remove all the contents of the pregnancy.

We drove home in silence. The radio was playing softly, Brian asked if I was going to call my mom. I said, "not yet." I needed time to process it. When we got home, I went to our theater room and found something funny to watch. I finally called Momma and sister Kathy. I told them I was all right when really, I was not, and I could hear that they were not either. This time was different. This time there was no busy schedule, no move, no unpacking, no business as usual. This time it was just me, my husband, and broken hearts. I just checked out emotionally. I did not want to talk or be around anyone. I just wanted to eat and watch television. I was uninterested in the next steps or learning why my body rejected the baby again.

My reality was I am not going to be a mother. God is not going to bless me with my own child. My nurse could tell in our conversation that I was struggling. She recommended therapy and gave me the name of someone who deals with women who cannot conceive or who have had miscarriages. I agreed that I needed to talk to someone besides my family and Brian. I was broken inside and needed help! This pain was like nothing I had ever experienced.

Two days before my scheduled D&C, I woke up in the middle of the night in pain and saw some light bleeding. I knew that I was losing the remains of my pregnancy. I did not wake Brian. Instead, I just went into our bathroom and closed the door. I got in the shower and just cried and went through the process alone. This time I felt all the emotions, not just from the current loss, but also from my previous losses. I had lost my sister, who was my connection to my Daddy, the year before. I had lost two children now. This felt like the night from hell!

I waited until morning to wake Brian up. When I told him what happened, he was quiet. I just crawled in bed with him, and we laid there together. As usual, he began talking optimistically. I didn't have much to say. I was physically and emotionally drained. I had once again checked out.

That was my state of mind for the next few weeks. I didn't talk to Brian, Kathy nor Momma about how I was feeling. My mom called me and said, "you really need to talk to someone. You are not dealing with your loss and with the social media attacks, you are sinking into a depression." I listened but didn't say much. I was emotionally deflated. One day, I asked Kathy to please schedule me an appointment with the psychiatrist that the doctor's office recommended.

In my first meeting, she helped me realize that what I was experiencing was grief. Not only was I grieving, but it was normal. She explained how some people didn't understand that miscarriages are indeed the loss of a child. That is when it hit me that I was mourning for two children, not just one. I had also just loss my sister the year before. Of course, I'd be overwhelmed with grief. She encouraged me to do some activities and take some time to allow myself to go through the stages of grief. I was a little surprised when the doctor suggested I find a way to memorialize my babies. I thought that was a good idea, but I didn't know what that would look like for me, so I had to think about what I would do now.

When I was able to talk about what had happened, I shared my psychiatrist's suggestion with my friend Alysia. A few days later, she gave me a beautiful Pandora bracelet with charms for my babies. I then added some of my own. Every day when I look down at my bracelet, I get to remember my babies. They were real! They were a part of me, and I don't have to act like I was never pregnant. It was okay for me to be sad, and I was. I didn't owe others an explanation. If I wasn't ready to share what I was going through or what my next steps were, it was okay and my choice completely.

I did start to feel better and open more to Brian and my family about my pain. They were all incredibly supportive. Listen, God knows what we always need. Yes, I had lost my babies, but my baby on earth is Bricen, and he was getting ready to graduate from high school. I threw myself into helping him prepare for graduation. I was so proud of him. He is truly one of the most caring, honest, and loving human beings I know.

I wanted to make sure we celebrated his accomplishment. I started planning his party, and I was so excited, but then it hit me. I needed to make sure his mother didn't have plans. Would he be staying with us after graduation or going back home with her for the summer? Did Bricen have a limited number of tickets for graduation? If so, was I going to be able to attend? All those questions sent me back into a deep state of depression. I am not his biological mother. I don't have children with my husband.

I took a deep breath and started asking everyone what the plans for Bricen were. Are there any plans? How can I be a part of the planning? Fortunately, his mother, and of course Brian, didn't have any problems with me taking the bull by the horns and running with it. That became my source of light for the next couple of months. When I tell you that was one of the best family days of my life! I was so happy for Bricen! The laughter from him and his friends was priceless.

Shortly before graduation, we started planning for another transfer. Honestly, this one didn't feel relevant. I had lost my will power to be excited or hopeful. I didn't pray about it the way I did in the past. I wasn't hopeful at all. In fact, I had very little conversation with Brian and my Momma. It felt more like a procedure that just needed to get done because of the number of embryos remaining. I was down to three embryos, and the doctor wanted to use two this time. Translate that to… I had two more chances to become a mother with this program.

After my ten days of having no pregnancy symptoms, I took a test the day before going to get my official bloodwork done. Just as I thought, it was negative. I even told Brian he didn't have to go to the doctor's appointment. I would be fine, and I already knew I was not pregnant.

The doctor thought it would be best to have a meeting with me and Brian after my appointment, and we agreed. This conversation was different. He seemed really puzzled as to why I hadn't had a successful pregnancy. There was no explanation as to what the problem was. He did want us to consider how difficult my transfers had been with my tilted uterus. He suggested we insert a catheter for two weeks to prepare for the next transfer. He ran additional tests on Brian, and everything was normal. I'm sad to say that we had the seventh transfer with no success.

According to the bible, seven symbolizes completion. I believe in God's word. Does this mean that I need to stop pursuing this route to be a mother? Am I never going to be a mother? Should I give up on pursuing baby Cole? So many uncertainties. But one thing's for certain, I am going to have faith that the outcome is God's will. His will and his alone.

CHAPTER 16

I'M YOUR ONLY PAPA

Daddy was a "girl dad" until he took his last breath. A part of his protective nature was to let everybody, I mean everybody, know that he was not just my daddy, but Shay, Kathy's, Trinnett's, Trina's, Delores,' and April's dad too. He often said, "those are my girls" without giving anyone details. During one of our conversations before he passed, he said, "I'm your Papa and I'm your only Papa." I just shook my head, and he kissed my forehead.

Not only was I struggling to move on to a better and healthier place after losing my dad, but I also did not want Momma to move on from being his wife. Although I was married and living away from home, Momma decided to have foster girls live with her and Delores. Her natural gift of wanting to help other girls kicked in. I was okay with it because I didn't want her to be alone. My dad died in 2000, and Momma was a widow for 5 years. In early spring of 2005, I noticed a difference in her. I had started traveling and would take Momma with me, and we were becoming girlfriends which I never expected to happen. But she started sending me and my sister, Kathy, to voicemail when we would call. She was giggling in ways I had never seen before. She was happier than I had ever seen her. My foster sisters told me everything, including the fact that a man was calling the house. What man?

I could not wait to ask her about this new man! She told me it was an old friend. Not just an old friend but her high school sweetheart, Marvin. I had never heard of this man before! The version I knew of my parents were that Momma moved in with her aunt her senior year in Mulberry, FL. She met my dad who was a junior. He was a football star, and Momma was the new girl in town. They dated briefly but later after high school, she moved to Jacksonville, FL where she met Kathy's dad in barber school. They then moved to Vero Beach, FL After Momma divorced, she was on the greyhound bus moving back to Jacksonville, FL and the bus driver recognized her. He was my dad's high school friend, and he knew my dad had recently relocated to Jacksonville from Orlando. That is how they reconnected. But that story was clearly missing a few minor details!

Marvin Simpson was the reason Momma moved to Mulberry, FL! He was my mom's boyfriend throughout junior high and high school. Momma even named her baby sister, Marvetta, after him! He went to Tampa to play football after he graduated, and that's why Momma moved to Mulberry. But neither of them had transportation so they never saw each other. In all honesty, she connected with the man who was really in love with her. My dad loved Momma, but I can honestly say, and she can too, that he was not in love. I told you earlier how I felt about their relationship. They were this married, corporate, power couple, and I know that she will be the first to admit that now.

So, when Marvin came back into the picture, I saw a different side of Momma. She laughed all the time. Mama has always been a fabulous dresser, but this was different. She just did extra everything. When I saw her in blue jeans, I almost passed out. I had never seen Momma in jeans! Then it hit me. I was watching a woman who was in love and being loved. It was so painful for my heart, but I was happy for her at the same time. Mother being loved the way she deserved to be loved, made me see a flaw in my daddy. Even with that realization, I still fought the idea of her ever being married to anyone else. I fought Marvin being nice to me because I felt like I was betraying Daddy, and that was just not true. I didn't want a stepdad but then it happened.

Some might call it immature, but I just was not ready for Momma to be married to anyone else. I felt like she was breaking up with Daddy even though he was already gone. I kept thinking about what he said to me before he died. He said, "I'm your only papa" and, to me, he meant that for Mommy too. So, I was mad at her and her new love. I kept saying, "Well as long as they don't get married."

Kathy was shocked at my behavior, but she tried to prepare me for the fact that our mother was remarrying. There was no way to prepare me. I kicked and screamed like a two-year-old.

Momma and Marvin were not just dating, they were serious and wanted to spend their lives together. Ten months after reconnecting, they were headed down the aisle. They did not invite me to the wedding; they tricked me in to attending the wedding. Everyone knows that I never say 'no' to Kathy, so my lovely big sister set me up. When she asked me to come hang out with the family at my godparents' house for the weekend, I said yes. It never crossed my mind that I was on my way to a wedding.

When I drove up, everyone was dressed up, and there was an arch and chairs in the yard. "What is going on? "I shouted in between tears. We dared not raise our voice at Momma, but I did that day. I was out of control. "You can't marry him." Then I had the nerve to compare his money to Daddy's. Even though Daddy and Momma had some hard times in the end, I had lived a middle-class life and I wanted Momma to continue to live that way. I was saying all kinds of crazy stuff. I was just hurt that she was getting married. Kathy took my mess for about five minutes and then she cleared the room. She even kicked Momma out.

She gave me the look of death.

"No matter what you say or feel, this wedding is happening. Momma was happy. Get yourself together!" That was it!

I was attending a wedding, despite my objections.

I was so wrong about my stepfather! He was a wonderful man, and he made Momma so freaking happy. He was also a protector like Daddy. Not only did he love Momma, but Marvin also loved all of Momma's girls and grandchildren. He was not interested being a stepfather. He did all he could to be a father to us. The fact that we were grown did not matter to him. He did fatherly things with us and for us. Every time I came home, he would take my car to the carwash and make sure everything was okay before I got on the road again. He had a come-to-Jesus with Brian before we got married, and he continued to let Brian know he was Papa number two. What a beautiful person he had turned out to be!

Eleven years later, Marvin died from congestive heart failure. Momma was heartbroken, and we were too. It was so painful for me to watch her bury not one, but two husbands. But I learned a valuable lesson from her new love and new life. In fact, I learned two lessons. I learned to never judge people based on what someone else has been to you. I was judging my stepdad based on my father's wealth and success. I also learned that you are never too old to find love. Momma not only found love again, but she was also truly loved by a beautiful man in her lifetime. I look back on that now, and I know that love spreads to those who are open to loving others and being loved. With all of that said, I can honestly say that I feel blessed to have had two father figures in my lifetime.

Just out of pure love and respect for my Daddy's memory, I never called Marvin, Dad, or Daddy! I mean never because Jerome is still my only Papa!

CHAPTER 17

CIRCLE OF INFLUENCE

I learned at an early age that your friends and the people in your immediate circle can play a huge impact in how you think and how you choose to approach life. Even more so than your parents at times. There was Little Miss Katie in the neighborhood who would pick and choose when she wanted to play with me but there were limitations. I wasn't invited into her home or pool. But I also met some kids that turned out to be lifers. My friend, Aqueelah who lived two blocks over was always over to play. My parents would let me visit her house too and we played with dolls and would go swimming. My first few years in school, I attended Trinity, so we only played on the weekends. But when I transferred to Jax Heights Elementary, we saw each other daily. We would walk or ride our bikes to school together. We even decided to be patrol guards together in the fifth grade.

Before Trina and Trinnett, Aqueelah was my first God sister. We took on that title for each other. We were more than best friends; she was like family. She was raised by her mother because her father died when we were young. She and her mother were Muslim and at first, I didn't know what that meant. Momma was Christian and although my dad wasn't initially attending church, I still didn't know if it would matter to them. I'm happy to say that it didn't! Momma and dad opened their hearts and our home to Aqueelah and her family. Years later, when Aqueelah's mother learned that my father gave his life to Christ, she came over to congratulate him. She was happy that he had made the decision to live as a Christian. But the two of them formed a rather interesting bond. As my dad begin to study the bible and become what we deemed a scholar, he and Aqueelah's mother would have great debates. Never in anger but interpretation of what he read from the bible and what she read from the Koran. That was the first time that I realized that people could have different opinions, points of views, and even interpretation on religion, but still love each other regardless. Because these two would go at it for hours then laugh and hug each other goodbye.

I watched how some kids and even faculty would treat Aqueelah sometimes due to her faith. I didn't like it at all. She was strong and could always defend herself, but I found myself being protective of her too. That was the first test of my loyalty as a friend. Her mother started a club for us, and other friends called, Zora Girls. It was named after Zora Neale Hurston who was a black author and best known for the book, "Their Eyes were Watching God." She introduced me to black literature. She wanted us to all have balance knowing that we lived in a predominantly white neighborhood. She felt it was important that we were exposed to black arts. We had book reports, dances, and even field trips together.

My best friend in elementary and junior high was white. I'll call her Amy in the book. When I was in the second grade, we wanted to do everything together. Her mother and dad would let me stay over and she was always welcomed at our house. We loved to dance, sing, and go skating. We made up routines and would put on talent shows with Aqueelah. The beauty in our relationship was the innocence. That childhood innocence of race and ethnicity not mattering. We all did everything together. I remember Amy's parents putting her in clogging lessons and I wanted to do it so bad. My parents were hesitant but because of the sports limitations due to sickle cell, they agreed. Of course, I was the only black child in those classes. But honestly, I didn't care. I just wanted to have fun with my best friend - Amy and I knew we would rock those shows together!

Amy was protective of me just as I was about her. There were a few neighborhood kids who didn't understand why she was my best friend, but she would let them have it! After a few years of clogging, I decided to quit but Amy kept going and became a rockstar with it. We remained good friends throughout junior high but when I transferred to Ed White

High School, we didn't stay in touch with each other. That's when Keyona and I became good friends. What I learned from each of these relationships is that who they were was rubbing off on me and vice versa. Our styles, music, choice of clothing, validation of boys, everything was discussed with each other. What they thought and what I thought mattered to each other. The opinions of my inner circle were always considered.

At that age, I thought my parents were delusional and old fashion like most adolescents. So, acceptance from my peers became a goal. I have these conversations with my niece, Ava now. I want to know her friends and be around all of them. I watch their interactions. Who are the leaders? Who are the followers? Whose opinion matters more to her and why? I didn't know that my parents were gaging all of this when I was young. They loved my relationships because all my friends' parents required education to be a priority. If anyone didn't do well on a test, they didn't get to play. So, we all pushed each other to do well and study so our play dates weren't impacted. They were respectful because their parents required respect. Then in Junior high, I learned about faz girls. You read it right, FAZ, not fast. Those were the ones my parents didn't let spend the night and I couldn't spend the night with them. Momma didn't play about me hanging with what she called faz girls. If their clothing was too short, too tight, or too little, she would let me know. If she deemed them to be "boy crazy" it was a no go. She had a keen sense on who she felt was faz. Now I get it! Being a part of the village with my nieces and younger cousins. You can say what you want, and it may be old school, but it honestly impacted me in more ways than I realized. It made me aware of how to carry myself, and my perception of others. I consider my outward appearance as a woman and how I present myself to other people.

I kept these friends throughout high school and met a few more but I was never one to call someone a "friend" quickly. I had my circle and of course my sisters. I think having older sisters helped me to understand that "friendships" are rare. Just because you meet someone or have mutual friends doesn't make them your friend. There's a bond that must grow and be nurtured. There's a mutual level of trust, respect, empathy, and encouragement that must be considered. Plus, is this person going in the direction that I want to go, or can I take them with me where I'm going.

In the 10th grade, I met my girlfriend, Patricia. She was this cute quiet ninth grader. I couldn't tell if she was African American or Puerto Rican. That's how I introduced myself, "Hi, my name is Earica, what's yours? "Where are you from" She shared with me that she was from the Virgin Islands. That was cool! I had never met someone from the Virgin Islands.

We started hanging out and she joined my step club. That summer, my sister, Kathy needed a babysitter, and I was not interested so I recommended Patricia. They had met a few times at school events, and it all worked out. Patricia's mother agreed and that entire summer and the next, Patricia watched my nieces and nephew. They loved her! She became a part of our extended family. When I decided to start a new step club, The Limited 20, my senior year, Patricia agreed to be the Vice President. I knew that having her as VP meant she would return her senior year as President and continue with the club. Over the last 29 years, Patricia has remained a part of my extended family. She is that person that in some of my darkest moments, she feels me. She reached out to just let me know that she's there, she cares, and is thinking about me.

Having friends who can encourage you when you aren't strong enough on your own is vital. Sometimes people think strong people don't need anyone. That's not true! It's sad because we need someone and don't know how to ask for help. I'm learning to ask for help.

My freshmen year in college, the "friends" that I made were not my best choices. That was one of the reasons why I decided to move back home after my freshmen year. It was another reminder of why you shouldn't let everyone infiltrate your inner circle. People carry baggage, self-esteem issues, and even insecurities that you can't heal. But as a friend, you try to fix it. You want to fix them and make them whole. But in doing so, sometimes they will turn on you and now you are caught in an unexpected drama that you didn't sign up for. So, when I went back home, it was just me, April, my cousin, Alexis, and my best friend, Keyona. That was it for me! No new friends had become my slogan! But I started working for a bank as a teller and my manager was so fly! Let me explain. I was twenty, just finished cosmetology school and a junior in college. Still trying to decide what I wanted to do after college. My manager was a young, African American woman who drove an Acura and wore a suit every day. Her name was Jacquie, and she had her masters and led the top branch on the east coast. Yes! She was a BOSS!

After a couple of months of working for her, she took interest in my career goals. She invited me to dinner after work because she knew I lived in the area near her. She saw that I was a hard worker and would often catch me studying on the job. Jacquie took a vested interest in me and I'm so thankful for her to this day. She started giving me additional responsibilities outside of the normal teller duties. It was a test to see if I'd complain or want to learn more but I was always up for the challenge. The bank had a business casual dress code so I would often wear kakis and a bank logo polo. One day, she told all the staff that some Vice Presidents were coming to our branch at the end of the week. We were the top producing branch in the State. She privately had a conversation with me. I'll never forget it. She said, "you have an opportunity to shine when these executives arrive. Take it! Dress for the position you want and not the one you have. Don't be shy and make them remember your name." That was it! That was the moment that birthed confidence into me as a professional in ways I never imagined. Those words are what I remind myself of in every role. Every opportunity. Every meeting. OWN THE ROOM! You get one chance to make an impression, don't waste it!

Jacquie and I became great friends. She was in my first wedding and planned my bridal shower. I was at her house when Joe and I received the call about my dad dying. But we did hit a bump in the road of our relationship. When I decided to divorce my ex-husband. Jacquie and another friend disagreed with my decision. She felt like I was giving up too easily. EASILY? She had witnessed the last few years of infidelity and the pain that I experienced. But I knew she just loved us both as a couple and wanted to see us together. So that wasn't what caused our distance. After Hurricane Katrina, Jacquie and I had a conversation. She was clearly concerned about me and where I was going to land on my feet. But during that conversation she said something that broke me. She asked did I think it was God "punishing me for leaving my marriage." It was at that moment that I knew the dynamics of our relationship had changed. Someone who I confided in numerous times and that pushed me into advancing my career made me feel lower than I could imagine during one of the most difficult seasons in my life. It took years for Jacquie and me to recover from that conversation. But I now know that in that moment, her intensions were not to hurt me. She felt that she was being a voice of reasoning. She later realized how it came across and we have worked on our relationship. Our friendship was worth saving. The value we add to each other stretches far beyond one moment of miscommunication.

After moving to Atlanta, my focus was my career and enjoying my single life! One of my friends, T'Ronda, who I met through Keyona was living in Atlanta. T'Ronda and Keyona attended school together in Gainesville, FL. I was so glad that she was there and without hesitation she gave me a warm welcome to Atlanta. I had a few cousins who lived in the suburbs of Atlanta but after attempting to contact them a few times with little to no response to connect, I was done trying.

T'Ronda and I would go out to dinner every night when I wasn't with Brian. She worked in public health so sometimes she would travel for weeks internationally. I'd miss her while she was gone but once she came back, we would paint the town. I got married so young that I never experienced life as a single woman. This was my do over and T'Ronda was just what the doctor ordered. We went to concerts, plays, games, comedy clubs, you name it, and we did it. It didn't take either one of us too much convincing to throw on some clothes and meet up. We would go out and before we entered the building, we would give each other fake names for the night. We knew the Atlanta singles game and we were eager to participate.

T'Ronda taught me how to travel. Yes, I had done some traveling throughout the US and gone to Jamaica on my honeymoon but that was it. She was not afraid to pack a couple bags and go anywhere in the world. I admired that even while T'Ronda was busy with work and enjoying being single, she was always committed to higher education. Every time I turned around, T'Ronda was in some class or program to further her education or advance her career. It was sometimes intimidating but she kept me on my toes. I knew I needed to be well versed in politics and whatever news headline for the day. There were times when I had sickle cell crisis and really didn't want Momma or family to know or worry and T'Ronda would let me stay with her and she would nurse me back to good health.

In the spring of 2007, I met a beautiful soul named, Alysia. I was hiring for a position, and she interviewed for the job. I could tell by our initial conversation; she was smart and talented. Although she didn't have the experience needed for the job, I recognized immediately she would be fantastic. It was the same moment that Jacquie and I shared when I worked for her. I offered Alysia the job and after a bit of negotiation, she came on board. My VP was concerned because of her lack of experience. That just made me more vested in her success. I needed her to see what I saw. So, I started mentoring her. Through that process, we became great friends. She too had moved to Atlanta for a fresh start. My employer had a rule about hanging with employees as a manager. So, we would sneak around and meet for lunch.

Alysia reminded me so much of my sister, April. I would tell them both they were twins in another lifetime. She, her husband, and children have become family. While dating Brian, I could go to her house, and we would talk for hours. You know that friend who can talk you off the ledge? That voice of reason, that person that will listen to everything you have to say and allow you to vent and then calmly let you know you were wrong. That person for me is Alysia.

Alysia is my ultimate hustler friend. She's never been afraid to start various entrepreneur ventures. I am so proud of the business mogul that she has become, and thankful God placed her in my inner circle. Each failed pregnancy, she would send me a simple text. "I love you." It would come exactly when I

234

needed it. Over the years, she has learned that I'm not good at being protected because I'm usually the protector. But she has a way of making me pull back the layers even when I don't want to.

As Alysia and I were getting to know each other, I became acquainted with two other employees, Kimberly and Lakisha. Kimberly was a rising star in another department. I've got to be honest, when we first met, it was awkward. She worked in the accounting department, and I felt some of their practices were outdated. So, of course, I would challenge them. It would annoy Kimberly but after a few times we laughed and she would say, "you're right! That's so stupid!" We giggle about it now. From that point forward, I like to remind her that I'm always right! Kimberly has become my best friend and I'm the godmother to her son. She and her husband were there for me after I decided to sell my townhome when I was struggling financially. They offered a guest bedroom in exchange for my famous banana pudding. I giggle about it because literally, they asked for nothing else. It was hard for me during that time. Here I was earning all this money and needing a place to stay while trying to stay afloat financially. They never judged me they were just there.

Do you have that friend that you can call or text and simply say, "I'm so upset" or "I need help" and they say, "who I need cuss out" or "what you need me to do"? That's Kimberly no matter what time it is, I can call or text her, and she puts on her superwoman cape. Kimberly was diagnosed in 2018 with kidney failure. I was just moving from Atlanta to Alabama and changing careers. I was devasted because I felt I couldn't physically be there for her like she was there for me! My superwoman was sick and there was nothing I could do to help her. At least that's what it felt like. Even when she is struggling herself, she is available to make sure I'm okay. It's funny because I often fuss at her when I find out later, she was sick or having a bad day but doesn't say anything. She's that strong friend that doesn't like to show her weakness so I've got to drag her to some undisclosed location (spa) where she can freely share. When people use the term, "check on your strong friends," it's real! Because if you don't, they will struggle in silence and feel like they are alone. I try to be consistent when checking on Kimberly.

Lakisha worked in the HR department. At first, I thought she was a spy. I thought my boss was trying to get her connected to me to see if I was fraternizing with the staff. So, it took a few months for our relationship to blossom. Lakisha (Kisha is what we call her) is that soft friend. Well, that's the impression she gives you until you rub her the wrong way. She doesn't know how to tell anyone no so sometimes I do it for her. I've watched her work tireless hours, drive the distance in Atlanta traffic, go home and take care of her family, and if someone else calls her needing something, she will lose herself in others' problems. For years, I watched Kisha do her job and someone else's, all while smiling and being so gracious. I would get so upset with her because I needed her to see her value the way others saw it. Her heart is so pure, and she is one of the most caring individuals I've ever met.

So here I am with unexpected new girlfriends. This was never a part of my plan. But it was all God's plan for me. We were running around town, meeting each other for lunches and dinners after work. Enjoying our twenties in ATL! These women are not only my girlfriends, but they've become an intricate part of my family. I share the stories of all these women in this chapter because they are lifers. Meaning there has never been any doubt if we would grow old together. Yes, I've got other friends who I love and who love me. But there's something special about my circle of influence. What they think matter. Them showing up or not showing up matters. Regardless of what we have personally going on, I expect more from them than I do other friends. Meaning, I feel an obligation to support their dreams, goals, and passion. I also feel an obligation to say, "Yo! You're messing up! Get it together!" In return, I expect and appreciate the same level of accountability from them. Yes, there are some people who come into your life for a season, and you must recognize that. Maybe it was to introduce you to the love of your life. It was to get you that job or your foot in that door of a great opportunity. It might have been to just show you a fun time as you go through a stage of grief.

Yes, learning a friend has done something to you that changes the dynamics of your relationship can really hurt. I've been there! You thought that person was on your side. But you find out that they had ulterior motives. Once it's revealed, just move on. Continue to build with your inner circle and protect your bond. Water those relationships. As we have all matured and have other responsibilities, family, careers, etc., we must find time to spend with each other. My girlfriend Alysia calls it time currency. I know it can become difficult. Many of us live in different states but we do what we can to make time. To show up! Those are the moments when the clock stops, and you feel like it was just yesterday when you saw each other. If your circle of influence doesn't make you want to do better in life, or make you want to be a better human in society, find a new circle!

CHAPTER 18

MY LITTLE AVAS

I am blessed to have two teenagers in my house most of the time. Bricen lives with us, but my niece, Ava, is with us a lot too because she lives with Momma. Ava living with Momma is a blessing not just for Ava but for Momma. Yes, Ava's mother needed help, but I didn't want Momma to be alone after Marvin died. It is amazing how history repeats itself because their relationship is so much like Momma's relationship with all her girls. Ava and Momma saved each other. Ava saved me in many ways, because Ava and Bricen are my children in every way that matters.

Ava is a wonderful young lady! Both often spend the night with us, and it gives me extra time with her. I spend our time wisely because I know she will go off to college soon, and I will not have the same influence in her life that I have now. There's always a transition during the adolescent years when you start thinking you know more than the adults around you. Until those mid to late twenties and you realize they were right! Our little teen will be a woman with her own ideas and the freedom to live the way she wants to live. It is my prayer that she will choose wisely and not forget her young self. For now,

I just want to share my journey with her. It is my hope that my journey will help her to see all the things NOT to do and make good decisions at the same time. Most of all, I want to be a good listener. That is what I do when I am with Ava. I listen first and then I talk! By listening, I learn so much about her and her personality, without having to ask anything at all. I learn about her young self. We talk about things that my generation did not discuss with our parents.

Honestly, I was afraid to talk to my mom, and I hate that now, but it is a fact. I may have made better decisions in relationships and in other moments as a woman with her guidance and influence. Momma didn't do or say anything at made me afraid to talk. It was the way she was raised, and she just pass that along to her girls. Me... I want to hear about Ava's life and tell her about my young self and my growth from good and bad experiences. I want to know what's she's thinking and why she feels the way she does. In my early days, we just heard, "because I said so," which never resulted in me understanding why. Now I take the opportunity to explain to her and Bricen why I feel the way I feel or why I'm not in agreement with their decision. It helps them see things from a different perspective and analyze what the outcomes may be if they do things different. I promise you, explaining will get better results from a teenager than just saying "no" and walking away-communication is key.

I also wanted to build a safe place of trust for Ava. A judgement free zone where she can share anything with me, even if I don't agree with her. Ava is so much like me at when I was her age. She loves school and I loved school! She tries to participate in every activity that Momma will allow, and she's outgoing and competitive. The difference between us is, Ava sees the good in people first which is something I didn't do at that age. It is wonderful to see the good in people, but I do not want her to let people take her for granted. Her first instinct is to believe everyone is good and their intentions are good. It's even hard trying to persuade her when someone or a situation is not good and why. Luckily, she hasn't had her heart broken yet. She hasn't experienced a backstabbing friend yet. Not if, but WHEN it happens, I don't want her to be emotionally distraught.

When I was young, we had bullies in school, but this new generation has taken bullying to a new level. It sometimes makes it way to social media and then it can be an ongoing nightmare. That's what I'm trying to protect her from. I need her to understand every snapchat friend or TikTok follower is not her friend. Not just Ava, but all young people when it

241

comes to social media is a major concern for me. It should be a concern for all adults.

I just pray that Ava will come to me or any adult in our family if they are having problems with their peers and their fears. I want her to tell me her secrets even if it feels uncomfortable. I had Kathy, Trinnett, and Trina to trust with my secrets, and they were never too far away. I'm trying to create that same bond with Ava.

A few months ago, she decided to join the election at school to become the student body Vice president. Well, her little bestie was also running for the same position, and they had to fill out paperwork to enter the race. Ava did not receive her email that included the form, so she was waiting for her bestie/opponent to send her the information.

" No, no, no," I said when she told me that she was waiting for her bestie to send her the information. "Why would your opponent send you the paperwork? You are responsible for your own campaign." I wanted her to understand what competition really looks like. I carefully framed the conversation in a way she would understand that she could still be friends with the young lady and look out for herself at the same time. Those are the things that my sisters talked to me about all the time. I did not say I listened! I said they talked to me all the time. To my young self, I should have listened.

I need Ava to know that if an organization or circle is not accepting of her, she can create her own. Her own organization, her own choir, her own dance club. Young people you can create your own company and make yourself the president. That is what I want for Ava and all young people around the world to do. Create your own path! Do not let other people tell you where you belong. You have the power to create a safe space, not only for you, but for others too. It is called leadership my little darlings. Don't follow... Lead!

I have friends who talk about experiences from high school that still bother them today. Well, I do not even know the names of the girls who rejected me, but I remember the good friends that moved on with me to our new club. I remember those girls who are women now and some of my best friends. Not people I know but close friends, twenty-five years later.

There are so many things that happened to my young self that I know were wrong, but there is nothing like what I experienced in my first marriage. The most painful part of my life was not loving myself enough, I chose to marry someone who was showing me signs of rejection before the marriage had even begun. A man who did not love me like a man should love a woman. I was too worried about what others would say and how it would impact them not attending a 1.5-hour ceremony of falsehood! If I do not teach my niece anything else, I want her to know that was the biggest mistake Auntie E made in her life. I want Ava to know I said, "I am sorry" to my young self. That's right! I apologized to me! I had to forgive me for those five years of misery so that I could heal! Healing your young self is the beginning of a long road to recovery, but you will get there, with time and work.

You are probably thinking about how you will never tell young folks your business. It is important to acknowledge your mistakes, trials, and tribulations when you are talking to young people. As I stated in the paragraph above, you cannot just say, do not do this and do not do that. That "Do as I say, not as I do" did not work when I was a teen, and it will not work with Ava and Bricen. You must talk their language and help them to understand that you were not a perfect teen, nor are you a perfect adult.

There were people in my life when I was younger who I thought walked on water. Literally! So, it was difficult trying to meet their expectations of perfection. Little did I know they were not all perfect, and they too fell short sometimes. I wish

I knew and understood that when I thought they walked on water.

Let young people know that your journey is not their journey, and you do not want the same hurtful things to happen to them that you have experienced. They will have their own scars, but hopeful they can learn from your battle and make smarter choices.

And listen, my battle is not over. At age 45, there is still so much to do and more lessons for me to learn. This book is the first time I have just said it all aloud. I shouted out the good, bad and the ugly, and that was not easy, but it was necessary. Necessary so that I could not only embrace my healing but help you with yours. We can heal our young self and help the beautiful Ava's of the world.

I hope that my words will encourage you to love your young self. If you are my age or older, I pray that this book will encourage you to forgive your young self and use your experiences to help someone else. I hope that you will read something, just one thing, in this book that will start your journey, so you know that you can forge a path that will heal your heart if you do not know that you are enough. A healed heart is a healthy heart that will lead you to success in so many areas of your life. It led me to Atlanta, good friends, and a wonderful husband. Most of all, it led me to a closer relationship with the God who healed so much of me that was broken. It will happen for you! It will heal your young self and lead you to the new you. It will happen because we are enough. It will happen because all the broken pieces of your life were meant to create your purpose.

The late Jerome Alexander
My Daddy
He was such a handsome man
10/4/1943 – 02/20/2000
Earica Cole's personal collection

L-R Kathy, Shay, Momma,
and me in the middle.
Always on stage! Kathy's
college graduation
Earica Cole's personal collection

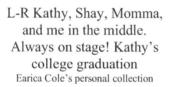

My parents wedding day
October 19, 1976
Earica Cole's personal collection

I was born Earica Alicia Alexander
Named after my mother Eara and my
grandmother (daddy's mom) Alice. I
was a cutie pie! Eleven toes and all!
Earica Cole's personal collection

Me and my daddy, Jerome Alexander
Daddy's girl!
Earica Cole's personal collection

Momma and I headed to church on
Easter in 1986
Earica Cole's personal collection

Family Christmas photo December 1997
Our last family photo before my dad passed in 2000.
Jerome Alexander Estate

Last Christmas photo with my stepdad, Marvin Tyrone Simpson,
L-R me, Marvin, Momma, Kathy, and Ava centered
Earica Cole's personal collection

My sisters and I minus April.
L-R Trinnett, Me, Shay,
Kathy, Trina, and Delores
Earica Cole's personal collection

Eara's Girls
L-R Trinnett, Me, April, and
Kathy. Eara centered
Jaleesa Lovely Productions

My beautiful sister, Terri
Alexander AKA Shay
May 18, 1972 – March 6, 2020
This picture represents who she
was. FSU Alumni and die-hard
FSU Football fan.
RIP – Shay
I love you!
Terri Alexander Estate

June 18, 2011
The day I married my best
friend, Brian Cole.
Pictured with Momma
Earica Cole's personal collection

Me and Bricen, my
bonus baby!
Earica Cole's personal collection

My family! Brian, Bricen, and I in 2022
Jaleesa Lovely Productions

Acknowledgements

I am thankful to God for everything! I'm nothing without him. I want to thank my husband, Brian for your continued support in all my dreams. You continue to be one of my biggest cheerleaders. Thank you, for allowing me to shine and never trying to dim my light or making me feel like we are in competition. I can only do what I do because you always have my back. Thank you to my mother for your love, teachings, and constant support. My big sister, Kathy...I love you! I could not have done this project without your partnership. God knew I would need you in every walk of my personal and professional pathways. To my late sister, Shay, I miss and love you dearly sis. Thank you for the laughs, love, and memories that we shared together. Our relationship wasn't perfect, but I pray that our story will help other siblings get it right. I also pray that I get the opportunity to get what we messed up right with your beautiful daughter. Thank you to my PR team (Jaleesa, Kelcy, and Vanessa). You all are amazing! We have grown to be family and you all challenge me daily to live the light God has given me in public. Thank you, Prophet Arnold McKay, for giving me confirmation from God that this was what I was supposed to do. You challenged me to go forth and how this was just the beginning of GREATER in my life. Lastly, to my family, friends, and followers on social media, who constantly support me and show up! I love you all! Thank you! Thank you! Thank you!

Made in the USA
Las Vegas, NV
17 January 2023

65779209R00149